superfoods
at **every meal**

superfoods
at every meal

Nourish Your Family WITH QUICK AND EASY RECIPES
USING 10 EVERYDAY SUPERFOODS

KALE • COCONUT OIL
• BLUEBERRIES • CHICKPEAS
• EGGS • QUINOA
• HONEY • SWEET POTATOES
• GREEK YOGURT
• WALNUTS

Kelly Pfeiffer

Fair Winds Press
100 Cummings Center, Suite 406L
Beverly, MA 01915

fairwindspress.com • quarryspoon.com

First published in the USA in 2015 by
Fair Winds Press, a member of
Quarto Publishing Group USA Inc.
100 Cummings Center
Suite 406-L
Beverly, MA 01915-6101
www.fairwindspress.com

19 18 17 16 15   1 2 3 4 5

ISBN: 978-1-59233-652-4

Digital edition published in 2015
eISBN: 978-1-62788-300-9

Library of Congress Cataloging-in-Publication Data available

Book and cover design by Rita Sowins / Sowins Design
Photography by Kelly Pfeiffer

Printed and bound in China

The information in this book is for educational purposes only. It is not intended to replace the advice of a physician or medical practitioner. Please see your health care provider before beginning any new health program.

*To my daughter, lovingly referred to as **Babycakes**. You inspire me daily to be my healthiest and happiest self and to follow my passions. I love you and can't wait to celebrate who you become.*

Contents

superfoods &
the nourished family

nour·ish

: to provide (someone or something) with food and other things that are needed to live, be healthy, etc.
: to cause (something) to develop or grow stronger.

—MERRIAM-WEBSTER'S DICTIONARY

As a mother and wife, I have three or four opportunities (i.e., meals) per day to nourish my family: to fuel their bodies to be healthy and strong and to help them be their best selves. What an awesome responsibility! Like most caregivers, I choose the food at the grocery store, I do the cooking, and I place the food on the table—usually trying to strike a balance between healthy and easy!

What this cookbook shows you is that you can (without much effort) provide nourishing foods—"superfoods"—at every meal. Not weird, obscure foods, but everyday superfoods you already know and love, such as eggs and nuts. Whether you're adding frozen wild blueberries to a breakfast smoothie, chickpeas to chocolate chip cookies, or Greek yogurt on a fish taco, every dish can include a powerful nutritional boost and still taste absolutely delicious.

I'm going to go out on a limb here and say that I'm probably not alone in this: my husband hates vegetables. I've seen him cringe—or worse yet, *sigh*—when he sees vegetables on his plate. If left to his own devices, he would probably live on pizza and cheeseburgers alone. But a couple of years ago, the same year that both his dad and his uncle had heart attacks in their fifties, my husband was diagnosed with high cholesterol and began daily medication to prevent a heart attack of his own.

This was the wake-up call both he and I needed. I had already changed my own diet, lost 50 pounds (22.7 kg), started a blog, and gone from obese to healthy, but while I made an egg scramble with kale, tomatoes, and garlic for myself, he was still eating a pepperoni pizza. While I snacked on Greek yogurt with fruit and nuts, he was devouring a bag of chips. You couldn't tell from his appearance, as he's always been naturally lean, but he wasn't healthy on the inside. I was making meals with superfoods, but he wasn't eating them.

After the diagnosis, however, I decided that I had to get more creative in the kitchen. I needed to make more of an effort to prepare dishes that included healthy foods that I knew he'd be more likely to not only enjoy, but finish. And that's where this book comes in. All of the recipes have been tested, devoured, and approved by my wonderfully picky husband, so if you have someone similar living in your household, fear not!

As for "Babycakes," my 4-year-old daughter, if left to her own devices and desires, she would subsist on the following: mac and cheese, PB&J, chicken nuggets, pancakes, bagels, and ice cream. She literally wakes up in the morning and the first thing out of her mouth is, "Can I please have ice cream?" So, it takes some extra effort to pack nourishing superfoods into her little body. The recipes in this book help me do just that. Knowing that she had kale and blueberries in her breakfast

smoothie, or Greek yogurt and chickpeas in her pancakes, makes sending her to school with her favorite peanut butter and jelly sandwich a little more palatable. I've also added superfoods to some of her favorite meals, such as Sweet Potato Mac & Cheese (page 133), Blueberry Creamsicles (page 167), and The Best Sloppy Joes (page 119). Adding healthy foods to your meals doesn't have to be hard or subtract from flavor. Stick with this book and you'll see just how easy it can be!

the 10 superfoods

The ten everyday superfoods in this book were chosen not only because of their well-known health benefits but also because of their extreme versatility, year-round accessibility, relative affordability, and overall appeal for most people. All are easily pronounced, and you've probably tried most of them before, though you may not have used them in such creative ways! In some recipes they are the main star; in others, they play more of a supporting role. Take sweet potatoes, for instance. In Maple Sweet Potato Hash with Fried Eggs on page 31, they play a leading role, and in All-Natural Pecan Pie on page 141, they are the supporting cast. Regardless, you are getting the nutritional boost in an absolutely delicious way that your entire family will love!

KALE

This cruciferous green veggie is gaining popularity, and for good reason. It is packed with vitamin K (more than 1,000 percent of the daily recommended value!), vitamin C (more than an orange!), vitamin A (more than any other leafy green!), calcium (more than a glass of milk!), and other antioxidants. It is great for your vision, immune system, bone health, metabolism, cholesterol levels, and even waistline. For all of the recipes in this book, I call for "de-stemmed" kale, meaning you cut off the thick stalks and use only the leaves. On its own it can taste a little bitter, but it is easily tamed when combined with either coconut oil or citrus or both. I prefer to buy organic kale when possible, because it's one of the crops that is often heavily sprayed with pesticides during the growing process.

COCONUT OIL

Coconut oil is made up primarily of saturated fat, a substance once avoided like the plague by health professionals. But coconut oil, now deemed a healthy saturated fat containing medium-chain fatty acids, actually reduces hunger *and* promotes higher fat burn—a one-two punch for weight management. It also lowers bad cholesterol while boosting brain function. Solid at room temperature (similar to butter), coconut oil melts into a liquid quite easily and is great for sautéing kale and sweet potatoes. The flavor is mild and in most recipes its presence is completely undetectable because of the small amount used. I prefer to buy and use virgin coconut oil (as opposed to refined coconut oil—the label is clearly marked), because more of the nutrients are kept intact this way.

BLUEBERRIES

Blueberries are bursting at the seams with antioxidants (more than any other fruit), vitamin C, and fiber. They help protect vision, increase brain function, reduce belly fat, and even boost heart health. Their sweet, mild flavor makes them super versatile, be it in smoothies, salads, or baked goods. As berries are one of the most highly sprayed crops, I recommend buying fresh organic berries in the spring and summer when the prices are reasonable (they're so much sweeter than the non-organic variety!) and then opting for frozen wild organic blueberries the rest of the year. This is one of the superfoods that my daughter will just munch on by itself, and frozen blueberries are one of her favorite lunchbox treats.

CHICKPEAS

Also known as garbanzo beans, chickpeas are a great source of both fiber and protein, and therefore excellent for hunger control. They have a delicious buttery flavor that is very versatile, but some people may find them chalky or bland. I often combat this by either adding chickpeas to soups or pureeing them with a liquid such as almond milk or sesame oil. I buy them canned for convenience reasons, but you can also buy them dried and then soak and cook them before use in these recipes. If you opt for canned, choose organic and thoroughly drain and rinse the beans to remove all the excess sodium.

EGGS

Once demonized for their possible link to higher cholesterol and heart disease, eggs are gaining in popularity now that it has been shown that they actually help *protect* against heart disease. They are also super satisfying, keeping you feeling full longer. The yolk contains most of their nutritional value, including B vitamins such as folic acid and choline, vitamins A and E, iodine, lutein, and protein, so some of the recipes in the book call for the yolk only. For maximum benefit, buy organic, cage-free eggs or get them from a local reputable source, if possible.

QUINOA

Pronounced *keen-wah*, this tiny seed contains all nine essential amino acids and is one of the most protein-rich foods you can eat. It is a seed, not a grain, and is entirely gluten-free. It's also full of iron, manganese, lysine, and riboflavin (B_{12}), which help with blood sugar control, weight management, brain function, and more. You can buy quinoa in a variety of colors: white, red, or tricolor. I tend to buy the red quinoa the most often, but choose whichever color is on sale, as quinoa can be pricey. The good news is a bag of quinoa multiplies once it is cooked: 1 cup (175 g) of dried quinoa becomes 4 cups (740 g) of cooked quinoa! You can cook quinoa on the stove top or in a rice cooker; just use the method that is most convenient for you.

Why Is It Important to Rinse Quinoa Before Cooking?

There is a detergent-like bitter coating on each quinoa seed, called *saponin*, that naturally protects the quinoa from birds and insects. If this is not rinsed before cooking, it can not only taste bad but cause stomachaches, or an even more severe allergic reaction in particularly sensitive people. Some quinoa brands note that they are "prewashed," which is great, but I still rinse it at least once anyway or until the water runs clear.

How to Rinse Quinoa

Quinoa seeds are so small that often a strainer isn't that helpful unless it's made of fine mesh. Instead, I add 1 cup (175 g) of quinoa to a 4-cup (940 ml) measuring bowl, then add water. Swish it around with a spoon (or your hand), let the quinoa settle a bit, and then carefully pour most of that water out. Repeat this process six or seven times, until the water finally runs clear. Note that you may lose a few of the quinoa kernels in the process, but it's worth it in the end.

HONEY

Honey is a great alternative to refined sugars, actually helping to regulate blood sugar based on its unique combination of fructose and glucose. It has anti-bacterial and anti-inflammatory properties, and is a great energy booster. The darker, raw, local honey is best, and many believe it may even help reduce seasonal allergies. This is cheaper when you buy more (or a larger size) at one time. Store honey at room temperature. It can crystallize if left for too many months, but it is still edible (just let it warm up in a bowl of hot water and stir well). Just as a reminder, it is not recommended to give honey to infants under the age of one because of the risk of botulism.

SWEET POTATOES

Boasting almost double the amount of fiber as regular potatoes, sweet potatoes are a true nutritional powerhouse. Their bright orange hue reflects their high beta-carotene and vitamin C content. But that's not all: they're also rich in vitamin D, iron, potassium, calcium, and manganese. Sweet potatoes work well in *any* meal—including desserts!—and are such a family-friendly food that I like to consider them the ambassadors of the vegetable world. I love baking a big batch at the start of the week and using them for different dishes every day.

GREEK YOGURT

Full of calcium, B vitamins, potassium, probiotics (good for digestion), and zinc, the Greek variety ups the ante over regular yogurt by delivering almost twice the protein content, helping you feel full longer. It is also thicker and creamier, creating a more indulgent experience. To get the most creaminess and dietary benefits, I suggest using full-fat (or 2 percent at the least) and avoiding the nonfat variety altogether. Additionally, all of the recipes in this book use plain *unsweetened* Greek yogurt for two reasons: first, it is more readily available in more places, and second, the recipes will stay consistent as far as sweetness goes, and using an already sweetened variety could make the final dish overly sweet.

WALNUTS

There's almost too much to write about this amazing nut! Full of antioxidants, omega-3 fatty acids, B vitamins, protein, folate, and more, walnuts help prevent heart disease, assist in weight management, help lower diabetes risk, improve brain function, aid in a good night's sleep, make your skin glow, strengthen your hair, and even help reduce stress. Walnuts are one of the cheaper nuts, compared to pistachios or hazelnuts, but the price can still add up quickly. I suggest buying walnuts in bulk so the price per ounce is the most reasonable. The smaller the bag you buy and the smaller the walnut is chopped, the more expensive, so it makes sense to buy big and prep it yourself.

I dislike chopping walnuts on a cutting board because the little pieces always seem to fly in a hundred different directions, so instead I put the walnuts into a sealed zip-top bag and then use the flat side of my meat tenderizer to crush them. Store your walnuts in the fridge to keep them the freshest, or even the freezer if you'll be keeping them for longer than a month. I always seem to use up my stash quicker than that, though!

breakfast &
brunch

Start your day off right with these superfood-packed breakfast options. From smoothies, to pancakes, to tacos, to quiches, I have you covered for easy, everyday breakfasts as well as leisurely weekend brunches.

Greek Yogurt Blueberry Banana Bread

★ Honey ★ Eggs ★ Greek Yogurt ★ Blueberries

This is one of my all-time favorite recipes. Absolutely moist and delicious, this banana bread is perfect for a leisurely weekend brunch at home or to bring to a gathering. Try using strawberries in place of the blueberries for a yummy alternative.

1¾ cups (210 g) unbleached all-purpose flour

1 tablespoon (14 g) baking powder

½ teaspoon sea salt

½ cup (100 g) coconut sugar

¼ cup (80 g) honey

1 teaspoon pure vanilla extract

1 cup (225 g) mashed bananas

2 eggs

¾ cup (172 g) plain Greek yogurt

1 cup (155 g) organic blueberries

Preheat the oven to 375°F (190°C, or gas mark 5). Spray a 9 x 5 x 3-inch (23 x 12.5 x 7.5-cm) loaf pan with nonstick spray.

Combine the flour, baking powder, salt, and sugar in a small mixing bowl. Stir thoroughly.

Combine the honey, vanilla, bananas, eggs, and Greek yogurt in a large mixing bowl. Stir thoroughly, then add in the dry mixture. Stir to combine. Fold in the blueberries.

Pour the batter into the prepared pan. Bake for 60 minutes, or until golden brown and a skewer inserted into the center comes out clean. Let cool in the pan before turning out onto a wire rack to cool completely.

YIELD: ONE 9 X 5 X 3-INCH (23 X 12.5 X 7.5-CM) LOAF

MAKE IT IN ADVANCE

I often bake this bread the night before and serve it the following morning for breakfast or brunch. Simply let the loaf cool in the loaf pan for an hour after baking, cover it with foil, and refrigerate overnight. It makes slicing the bread much easier and makes mornings a breeze!

Blueberry Pancakes

Chickpeas ∗ *Greek Yogurt* ∗ *Honey* ∗ *Eggs* ∗ *Blueberries* ∗ *Coconut Oil*

This is our go-to pancake recipe. The pancakes are full of nourishing superfoods and yet are perfectly light and fluffy! Everyone in the family loves them. Use this recipe as a base and try other flavors in place of the blueberries, such as strawberries, peaches, cinnamon, or even canned pumpkin.

⅔ cup (160 g) chickpeas,
    rinsed and drained

½ cup (115 g) plain Greek yogurt

¼ cup (85 g) honey

1 cup (120 g) unbleached all-
    purpose flour

1½ teaspoons baking powder

2 eggs

¾ cup (112 g) organic blueberries,
    frozen or fresh

1 teaspoon coconut oil

Combine the chickpeas, Greek yogurt, and honey in a large measuring cup. Use an immersion blender—a blender or food processor will also work—to puree until smooth. In another bowl, combine the flour and baking powder.

Add the chickpea mixture and eggs to the flour mixture and stir to combine. Fold in the blueberries.

In a skillet over medium-low heat, melt the coconut oil. Once hot, scoop the pancake batter onto the skillet, leaving room between each pancake. Once bubbles appear on top, flip the pancakes and cook on the other side, being sure to brown both sides evenly.

YIELD: 8 PANCAKES

superfoods *at every meal*

Banana Nut Pancakes

❋ Greek Yogurt ❋ Eggs ❋ Walnuts ❋ Coconut Oil

It's like a banana nut muffin in pancake form! I love making a double batch so that we can freeze the extras and eat them throughout the week. If you don't have coconut sugar, a natural sugar with a rich brown color and flavor, use regular sugar.

¾ cup (172 g) plain Greek yogurt

1 egg

1 teaspoon coconut sugar

¼ cup (60 ml) vanilla almond milk or plain almond milk

1 teaspoon pure vanilla extract

½ banana, mashed

¾ cup (90 g) unbleached all-purpose flour

½ teaspoon baking soda

½ teaspoon baking powder

½ cup (60 g) coarsely chopped walnuts

1 teaspoon coconut oil

In a mixing bowl, combine the yogurt, egg, coconut sugar, almond milk, and vanilla with a whisk. Add the banana and stir until smooth.

In a small bowl, sift together the flour and baking soda and powder. Add to the yogurt mixture and stir to combine. Fold in the walnuts.

In a skillet over medium-low heat, melt the coconut oil. Once hot, scoop the pancake batter onto the skillet, leaving room between each pancake. Once bubbles appear on top, flip the pancakes and cook on the other side, being sure to brown both sides evenly.

YIELD: 8 PANCAKES

DIPPING VS. DROWNING

I've found that my daughter consumes significantly less maple syrup if I cook her silver dollar–size pancakes that she can dip by hand into the maple syrup. Otherwise, she's begging me multiple times during breakfast to pour more syrup on top of her already drowning pancakes. Try it with your kids (or adults!) by using small ramekins or dipping bowls.

Blueberry Crumble Muffins

* Chickpeas * Greek Yogurt * Honey * Eggs * Blueberries

Say goodbye to muffins from a box . . . for good. These are so easy to put together and so much better for you!

FOR MUFFINS:

⅔ cup (160 g) chickpeas, rinsed and drained

½ cup (115 g) plain Greek yogurt

¼ cup (80 g) honey

2 cups (240 g) brown rice flour or unbleached all-purpose flour

1 teaspoon baking powder

1 teaspoon baking soda

¼ cup (60 ml) vanilla almond milk

2 egg whites

2 teaspoons pure vanilla extract

¼ cup (50 g) coconut sugar

¾ cup (112 g) organic blueberries, fresh or frozen

FOR CRUMBLE TOPPING:

2 tablespoons (16 g) brown rice flour or unbleached all-purpose flour

2 tablespoons (28 g) unsalted butter

2 tablespoons (24 g) coconut sugar

Preheat the oven to 375°F (190°C, or gas mark 5). Spray the cups of a muffin tin with nonstick spray.

To make the muffins: Combine the chickpeas, Greek yogurt, and honey in a large measuring cup. Use an immersion blender—a blender or food processor will also work—to puree until smooth.

In a large bowl, add the flour, baking powder, and baking soda and whisk to combine. Add the blended chickpea mixture, almond milk, egg whites, vanilla, and sugar and stir to combine. Fold in the blueberries.

Pour the batter into the muffin cups, dividing it evenly.

To make the topping: Mix together the flour, butter, and coconut sugar in a small bowl. Press a small spoonful of the crumble mixture onto each muffin with your fingers or the back of a spoon.

Bake for 25 minutes, or until a toothpick inserted into the center of a muffin comes out clean.

YIELD: 12 MUFFINS

TOPPING OPTIONAL

Feel free to omit the crumble topping if you are trying to reduce calories. These muffins are still great without it!

Sweet Potato Muffins with Walnut Streusel

* Sweet Potatoes * Coconut Oil * Walnuts

These flavorful sweet potato muffins are topped with a decadent crumble topping made of walnuts, coconut sugar, and butter. You will definitely want to go back for seconds and maybe thirds.

FOR MUFFINS:

1 large sweet potato, cooked and mashed

¾ cup (180 ml) vanilla almond milk

½ cup (112 g) coconut oil, melted

¾ cup (150 g) coconut sugar

2 cups (240 g) unbleached all-purpose flour

1 tablespoon (14 g) baking powder

2 teaspoons ground cinnamon

¼ teaspoon ground cloves

½ teaspoon ground ginger

FOR CRUMBLE TOPPING:

½ cup (60 g) chopped walnuts

2 tablespoons (24 g) coconut sugar

2 tablespoons (28 g) unsalted butter

1 teaspoon ground cinnamon

Preheat the oven to 400°F (200°C, or gas mark 6). Spray the cups of a muffin tin with nonstick spray.

To make the muffins: Add the sweet potato, milk, coconut oil, and sugar to a large mixing bowl. Stir until thoroughly combined.

In a separate bowl, combine the flour, baking powder, cinnamon, cloves, and ginger. Whisk to combine. Add to the wet ingredients and stir to combine.

Pour the batter into the muffin cups, dividing it evenly.

To make the topping: Mix together the walnuts, coconut sugar, butter, and cinnamon in a small bowl. Press a small spoonful of crumble onto each muffin.

Bake for 30 minutes, or until a toothpick inserted into the center of a muffin comes out clean.

YIELD: 12 MUFFINS

COOKING THE SWEET POTATO

Either bake the sweet potato (sliced in half) for 1 hour in a 400°F (200°C, or gas mark 6) oven or cook whole in a microwave on high for 5 minutes. Whatever you do, don't boil the sweet potato because it will retain too much water and make the muffins mushy—lesson learned from experience!

Honey Biscuits & Blueberry Jam

✱ Honey ✱ Blueberries

These biscuits, sweetened with just a bit of honey, are the perfect backdrop for a dollop of home-made jam. This is called "refrigerator jam," different from jam that you preserve in jars, because it is super easy to make, contains zero pectin, and stores nicely in the fridge for a week or two.

FOR BISCUITS:

2 cups (240 g) unbleached all-purpose flour

1½ tablespoons (21 g) baking powder

1 tablespoon (20 g) honey

6 tablespoons (84 g) cold unsalted butter, plus 1 tablespoon (14 g), melted, for brushing tops

¾ cup (180 ml) milk

FOR JAM:

2 cups (310 g) organic blueberries

⅔ cup (132 g) coconut sugar

⅓ cup (106 g) honey

1 tablespoon (8 g) cornstarch

Preheat the oven to 450°F (230°C, or gas mark 8).

To make the biscuits: In the bowl of a food processor, combine the flour, baking powder, honey, cold butter, and milk. Blend until thoroughly combined. Remove the dough from the food processor, and knead it approximately 10 times on a flat surface. Pat the dough flat, keeping it about 1 inch (2.5 cm) thick.

Use biscuit cutters or cookie cutters to cut the dough into circles (or hearts). Place the biscuits on a nonstick cookie sheet. Brush the melted butter on top of each biscuit.

Bake for 10 minutes, or until lightly browned.

To make the jam: Combine the blueberries, sugar, and honey in a medium-size saucepan over medium heat. Let simmer for approximately 10 minutes, until completely softened and combined. Add the cornstarch, stirring continuously until there are no clumps of cornstarch left. Serve warm, or refrigerate until ready to serve.

YIELD: 12 BISCUITS & 1½ CUPS (480 G) JAM

Perfect Scrambled Eggs

✱ Coconut Oil ✱ Eggs

The secret to perfect scrambled eggs every single time is twofold: 1) melting coconut oil in the pan before adding the eggs, and 2) cooking/stirring them over medium-low heat. They stay perfectly fluffy and don't stick to the bottom of the pan!

1 tablespoon (14 g) coconut oil

6 eggs

¼ cup (30 g) shredded white Cheddar cheese

In a skillet over medium-low heat, melt the coconut oil. Crack the eggs into the pan and add the cheese, stirring to scramble. Cook for 4 to 5 minutes, until the eggs are cooked through.

YIELD: 3 SERVINGS

Yogurt Power Parfait

* Greek Yogurt * Chickpeas * Honey * Coconut Oil * Blueberries * Walnuts

This is an on-the-go breakfast at its finest. Throw five ingredients into a bowl, stir, and devour the protein-packed, antioxidant-rich goodness! Or pack it up to enjoy later in the day.

¾ cup (172 g) plain Greek yogurt

¼ cup (95 g) Chickpea Nut Butter (opposite) or peanut butter

½ cup (75 g) organic blueberries, fresh or frozen

¼ cup (30 g) chopped walnuts

¼ cup (30 g) blueberry granola

Combine all the ingredients in a bowl. Stir. Devour.

YIELD: 1 SERVING

Chickpea Nut Butter

* Chickpeas * Honey * Coconut Oil

I use this nut butter for everything! Slather it on toast, make a pb&j sandwich, put it in a yogurt parfait (opposite), make a peanut dipping sauce out of it, or just eat it by the spoonful.

1 cup (240 g) chickpeas, rinsed
    and drained
1 cup (260 g) peanut butter,
    preferably unsweetened
2 tablespoons (40 g) honey
2 tablespoons (30 ml) peanut oil
1 tablespoon (14 g) coconut oil,
    melted
1 teaspoon pure vanilla extract

Combine all the ingredients in a food processor. Blend thoroughly. Refrigerate whatever you don't use.

YIELD: 2 CUPS (570 G)

Maple Sweet Potato Hash with Fried Eggs

* Sweet Potato * Coconut Oil * Eggs

Really, what's not to love about a big ol' plate of sweet potatoes covered in maple syrup? Paired with fried eggs and dried apricots, this dish is the perfect combination of savory and sweet. If you don't have any dried apricots on hand, feel free to use another fruit (even fresh), such as pears, apples, or golden raisins.

1 tablespoon (14 g) coconut oil

1 sweet potato, peeled and diced

2 tablespoons (10 g) diced yellow onion

3 tablespoons (45 ml) dark amber pure maple syrup

2 tablespoons (18 g) diced dried apricots

⅛ teaspoon ground cinnamon

⅛ teaspoon sea salt, plus more to taste

2 to 4 eggs, depending on servings

Freshly ground black pepper

In a skillet over medium-high heat, melt the coconut oil, then add the sweet potato and onion. Sauté for approximately 8 minutes, until the sweet potatoes are softened.

Add the maple syrup, apricots, cinnamon, and salt, stir to combine, and sauté until lightly browned, about 4 minutes. Remove from the pan and transfer to 2 to 4 serving plates.

Crack the eggs into the hot skillet (no need to wipe out), cover with a glass lid, and cook for 2 to 3 minutes for a runny yolk, or 4 to 5 minutes for a firmer egg. The egg whites should be opaque. Season with salt and pepper and slide an egg over each serving of hash. Serve immediately.

YIELD: 2 TO 4 SERVINGS

SERVING SUGGESTION

Try adding some diced ham or bacon for the meat lovers in your house, or serve with toasted bread. Either would be delicious!

Ham & Feta Quiche in a Quinoa Crust

★ Quinoa ★ Greek Yogurt ★ Eggs

Sophisticated, savory, and hearty, this quiche has a bit of Greek flair with the feta, cucumber, and yogurt. And did I mention it bakes up beautifully? Your friends and family will be impressed!

FOR CRUST:

2 cups (370 g) cooked quinoa

¾ cup (90 g) unbleached all-purpose flour

1 teaspoon garlic powder

2 tablespoons (10 g) grated Parmesan cheese

½ cup (1 stick, or 112 g) cold unsalted butter

FOR FILLING:

6 eggs

½ cup (115 g) plain Greek yogurt

¼ teaspoon black pepper

1 cup (150 g) diced, smoked ham

½ cup (60 g) diced cucumber

¼ cup (15 g) chopped fresh parsley

½ cup (75 g) crumbled feta cheese

Preheat the oven to 400°F (200°C, or gas mark 6). Spray a 9-inch (23-cm) pie pan with nonstick spray.

To make the crust: Combine all the crust ingredients in a medium-size mixing bowl. Mash together with a fork until thoroughly mixed. Press the quinoa crust mixture into the pan so that it's evenly covered, and then bake the crust by itself for 10 minutes.

To make the filling: Whisk the eggs, yogurt, and pepper together in a medium-size mixing bowl. Add the ham, cucumber, parsley, and feta cheese and stir to combine.

Once the crust has baked for 10 minutes, pour in the filling. Return to the oven and bake for an additional 40 minutes, or until the eggs are set and the top is golden brown.

YIELD: ONE 9-INCH (23-CM) QUICHE; 8 SERVINGS

RECIPE PAIRINGS

When I buy more unusual ingredients—such as feta, for example—I like to have a couple of recipes on hand to make that week so that none of it goes to waste. Use any leftover feta from this quiche recipe to make my 7-Layer Greek Dip on page 51.

Kale & Cauliflower Crustless Quiche

* Coconut Oil * Kale * Eggs

Babycakes and I like to enjoy a patio picnic with this quiche and pair it with a piece of toast smothered in homemade jam. She devours every veggie-laden bite of the quiche and even asks for seconds.

2 tablespoons (28 g) coconut oil
½ cup (35 g) chopped de-stemmed kale
1 teaspoon minced garlic
2 cups (200 g) diced cauliflower
½ cup (75 g) diced ham
⅓ cup (40 g) grated Cheddar cheese
⅓ cup (40 g) grated Swiss cheese
6 eggs
⅓ cup (80 ml) milk
1 teaspoon sea salt
¼ teaspoon black pepper

Preheat the oven to 350°F (180°C, or gas mark 4). Spray a 9-inch (23-cm) pie pan with nonstick spray.

In a skillet over medium heat, melt the coconut oil, then add the kale and garlic. Sauté for approximately 5 minutes, then transfer to a mixing bowl. Add the cauliflower, ham, and cheeses and stir to combine. Pour into the prepared pie pan, spreading evenly.

In a mixing bowl, whisk together the eggs, milk, salt, and pepper. Pour over the vegetables in the pie pan, pressing down with a fork to make sure the egg covers everything.

Bake for 1 hour, or until the eggs are set and the top is golden brown.

YIELD: ONE 9-INCH (23-CM) QUICHE, OR 8 SERVINGS

PREFER CRUST?

A crust is not necessary for delicious quiche. But if you like the look and feel of a quiche with crust better, try my quinoa crust recipe on page 32, parbaking it first as directed.

Kale Egg Scramble

* Coconut Oil * Kale * Eggs

Ready in just five minutes, this is one of the quickest and simplest breakfasts to make. We have it at least once a week! Double or triple the amounts to make it family-size.

1 teaspoon coconut oil

1½ cups (105 g) chopped, de-stemmed kale

1 teaspoon minced garlic

8 grape tomatoes, halved

2 eggs

1½ teaspoons milk

Crumbled goat cheese, for sprinkling on top (optional)

In a skillet over medium heat, melt the coconut oil. Add the kale, garlic, and tomatoes. Sauté for approximately 5 minutes, until soft. Push the sautéed veggies to one side of the skillet to make room for the eggs.

Crack the eggs into a bowl, add the milk, and whisk to combine. Pour into the skillet and stir frequently until the eggs are cooked through and no longer translucent, 3 to 4 minutes.

Sprinkle the goat cheese on top of the scrambled eggs and serve with the sautéed veggies.

YIELD: 1 SERVING

Quinoa Breakfast Tacos

* Coconut Oil * Eggs * Quinoa * Greek Yogurt

I absolutely love Mexican food, and breakfast is no exception! These tacos will get your morning off to a great start.

FOR FILLING:

1 tablespoon (14 g) coconut oil

4 eggs

1 cup (185 g) cooked quinoa

2 tablespoons (30 g) black beans

2 tablespoons (32 g) salsa

1 tablespoon (1 g) chopped fresh cilantro

FOR SAUCE:

½ cup (115 g) plain Greek yogurt

Juice of ½ lime

8 corn tortillas

To make the filling: In a skillet over medium heat, melt the coconut oil. Add the eggs, quinoa, beans, salsa, and cilantro. Stir to scramble and cook until the eggs are set.

To make the sauce: Combine the yogurt and lime juice in a small bowl, stirring well.

Fill each corn tortilla with a heaping scoop of the egg mixture, then top with the Greek yogurt sauce.

YIELD: 8 TACOS

Blue Power Smoothie ➺

❋ Kale ❋ Honey ❋ Blueberries

This is a powerful way to start your morning and get your greens without even tasting them! The sweetness of the blueberries and honey completely hides the flavor of the kale. Babycakes happily drank an entire glass and begged for more! That's my kind of morning.

1 cup (235 ml) vanilla almond milk

2 cups (140 g) chopped de-stemmed kale

2 tablespoons (40 g) honey

1 cup (155 g) frozen organic blueberries

1 banana

1 cup ice

Combine all the ingredients in a blender. Blend until smooth. Serve immediately.

YIELD: 3 CUPS (705 ML)

Banana Cream Protein Smoothie

❋ Chickpeas ❋ Honey ❋ Greek Yogurt ❋ Walnuts

This tastes similar to a creamy peanut butter smoothie but with the benefit of more fiber and protein! My husband had no idea there were chickpeas in it, and I didn't mention it. He'll find out when he reads this book!

1 cup (240 g) chickpeas, rinsed, drained, and frozen

2 tablespoons (40 g) honey

1 cup (230 g) plain Greek yogurt

⅔ cup (80 g) chopped walnuts

1 banana

1 apple, peeled and cored

⅔ cup ice

Combine all the ingredients in a blender. Blend until smooth. Serve immediately.

YIELD: 3 CUPS (705 ML)

FREEZING CHICKPEAS

Whenever I have a recipe that calls for only a partial can of chickpeas (such as the Blueberry Crumble Muffins on page 23, for instance), I throw the rest into a zip-top bag and freeze them to use in smoothies. And if you don't have any frozen for this recipe, no worries: unfrozen can be used in a pinch.

← Green Monster Smoothie

* Kale * Greek Yogurt * Honey

This smoothie, with its vibrant green color, is a bit monster-esque on the outside, but beautiful and sweet on the inside. Try adding a handful of peach slices or fresh mango in the summer!

2 cups (140 g) chopped
de-stemmed kale

1 banana, frozen

1¼ cups (295 ml) peach mango
  coconut water (or plain)

¾ cup (172 g) plain Greek yogurt

2 cups ice

1 tablespoon (20 g) honey

Combine all the ingredients in a blender. Blend until smooth. Serve immediately.

YIELD: 3 CUPS (705 ML)

Maple Nut Quinoa

* Quinoa * Walnuts

Quinoa for breakfast? Oh yes! When you layer it with chopped bananas, walnuts, and maple syrup, quinoa is transformed into the ultimate protein-packed breakfast food.

2 cups (370 g) cooked quinoa,
  cooled

2 tablespoons (30 ml) maple syrup

1 teaspoon pure vanilla extract

1 tablespoon (15 ml) vanilla
  almond milk

1 teaspoon ground cinnamon

¾ cup (112 g) chopped banana

½ cup (60 g) coarsely chopped
  walnuts

Combine the quinoa, maple syrup, vanilla, almond milk, and cinnamon in a medium-size mixing bowl. Stir to combine. Fold in the banana and walnuts. Serve cold.

YIELD: 3 SERVINGS

SUNDAY NIGHT PREP

I don't do a lot of traditional meal prepping on the weekends. However, I do try to make a batch of quinoa every Sunday night, so that I have cooked quinoa readily available to use in recipes (such as this one) throughout the week.

appetizers

These appetizers are worth throwing a party for. From crostini and dips to poppers and chips, there is something here for everyone. So go ahead and send out that invite!

Blueberry Bruschetta

* Blueberries * Honey

This is a perfect party-worthy appetizer. Its beautiful, vibrant colors and mouthwatering flavors are sure to be the hit of the party! Enjoy it on slices of toasted bread or by the spoonful. I won't judge.

¾ cup (112 g) organic blueberries, mashed

¾ cup (112 g) diced grape tomatoes

1 tablespoon (15 g) basil paste or 20 fresh basil leaves

1 tablespoon (20 g) honey, plus more for drizzling, if desired

¼ teaspoon sea salt

1 tablespoon (15 ml) olive oil

1 teaspoon white balsamic vinegar

Sliced bread (I use gluten-free millet chia bread)

Preheat the oven to 400°F (200°C, or gas mark 6).

Combine the blueberries and tomatoes in a medium-size bowl.

In a small bowl, combine the basil paste, honey, salt, olive oil, and vinegar, stirring well. (If using basil leaves, add them to the bowl with the berries.) Pour the dressing over the blueberries and tomatoes and toss gently to coat. Set aside.

Spread the bread slices on a cookie sheet and bake for 10 minutes. Remove from the oven, top each slice with a large spoonful of the bruschetta, and drizzle with additional honey.

YIELD: 18 TO 24 BRUSCHETTA PIECES, DEPENDING ON THE BREAD

AVOID SOGGY BREAD

To combat soggy bread with the blueberry bruschetta at a party where the appetizer might be eaten over an hour or more, serve the bruschetta in a bowl with a spoon and the toasted bread on the side. Then guests can make their own at the moment they're ready to eat it!

Quinoa Corn Poppers

※ Quinoa ※ Eggs ※ Greek Yogurt

These Quinoa Corn Poppers are a smashing success. They are great immediately out of the fryer, but also after an hour sitting on the counter at a party (on the slim chance there are any left!).

¾ cup (90 g) brown rice flour or unbleached all-purpose flour

½ teaspoon chili powder

½ teaspoon sea salt

1 (15-ounce, or 420 g) can organic sweet corn kernels, rinsed and drained

1 cup (185 g) cooked quinoa

2 tablespoons (18 g) diced jalapeños

½ cup (60 g) shredded Cheddar cheese

1 cup (225 g) ground chicken

2 egg yolks, slightly beaten

3 cups (705 ml) vegetable oil, for frying

¾ cup (172 g) Greek yogurt, for dipping

¾ cup (195 g) salsa, for dipping

In a small bowl, whisk together the flour, chili powder, and salt.

In a separate bowl, mix together the corn, quinoa, jalapeños, cheese, chicken, and egg yolks. Add the flour mixture and stir to combine.

Pour the vegetable oil into a deep fryer and heat to 375°F (190°C) on an instant-read thermometer. Place a few layers of paper towels on a plate.

Form the quinoa corn mixture into approximately 1½-inch (3.8-cm) balls, then carefully add in batches to the hot oil, being careful not to crowd the pot, and fry for 4 minutes. Remove with a spider or slotted spoon and drain on the paper towel–lined plate. Repeat with the remaining poppers, bringing the oil back to temperature in between batches.

Serve hot, with the Greek yogurt and salsa for dipping.

YIELD: 24 TO 30 POPPERS

Quinoa Bruschetta

Once you make this bruschetta, you will want to put it on everything! We eat it on toasted bread, over pasta with shrimp, or just by the spoonful.

1 cup (185 g) cooked quinoa, cooled

1½ cups (225 g) diced grape tomatoes

¼ cup (25 g) grated Parmesan cheese

1 tablespoon (15 g) basil paste or 20 fresh basil leaves

2 teaspoons minced garlic

2 teaspoons white balsamic vinegar

1 teaspoon honey

2 teaspoons olive oil

Salt and pepper, to taste

Gluten-free bagel chips or sliced French bread, for serving

Add the quinoa, tomatoes, and cheese to a small mixing bowl. Stir to combine.

In a separate bowl, combine the basil paste, garlic, vinegar, honey, oil, salt, and pepper and whisk to blend (if using basil leaves, add to the quinoa mixture). Pour over the quinoa mixture and stir to combine.

Serve with the gluten-free bagel chips or sliced French bread.

YIELD: 12 SERVINGS, OR APPROXIMATELY 3 CUPS (480 G)

Quinoa Pizza Bites

* Quinoa * Eggs * Coconut Oil

I don't know about yours, but my family LOVES pizza! And even though my husband was skeptical at first when he saw quinoa and zucchini in the mixing bowl, he devoured these little pizza bites.

¾ cup (90 g) unbleached all-purpose flour

1 teaspoon paprika

1½ teaspoons dried basil

½ teaspoon sea salt

1 teaspoon dry ranch dressing mix

4 eggs

2 cups (370 g) cooked quinoa

½ cup (60 g) shredded mozzarella cheese

½ cup (100 g) grated Parmesan cheese

2 teaspoons minced garlic

1 cup (120 g) diced zucchini

1 tablespoon (14 g) coconut oil, melted

⅓ cup (40 g) diced pepperoni (optional)

Pizza sauce, for dipping

Preheat the oven to 350°F (180°C, or gas mark 4). Coat 2 mini muffin tins with nonstick spray.

Whisk to combine the flour, paprika, basil, salt, and ranch mix in a large bowl.

In a separate bowl, whisk the eggs, and then add the quinoa, cheeses, garlic, zucchini, oil, and pepperoni, if using. Stir to combine. Add the flour mixture and stir well.

Fill each muffin cup with a spoonful of the quinoa mixture.

Bake for 20 minutes, or until lightly browned. Serve with the pizza sauce for dipping.

YIELD: 24 MINI PIZZA BITES

PERSONALIZED PIZZA TOPPINGS

Are your favorite pizza toppings sausage and peppers? Pepperoni and pineapple? Mushrooms and spinach? Feel free to get creative in the kitchen and top with your favorites.

Chipotle Cheesy Corn Dip

Greek Yogurt ∗ *Eggs*

This creamy dip has quite a kick. The addition of Greek yogurt cools things down a bit, while amping up the protein content. I love how easy it is to put this dip together and how quickly it gets devoured!

1 (15-ounce, or 420 g) can organic sweet corn kernels, rinsed and drained

⅓ cup (40 g) diced green chiles (I used mild)

1 cup (230 g) plain Greek yogurt

2 cups (240 g) grated pepper Jack cheese

2 egg yolks

½ teaspoon sea salt

1 tablespoon (9 g) minced sweet cherry peppers

1½ teaspoons minced chipotle peppers

Blue corn tortilla chips, for serving

Preheat the oven to 400°F (200°C, or gas mark 6). Coat a 9-inch (23-cm) pie pan with nonstick spray.

Add the corn, chiles, yogurt, cheese, egg yolks, salt, and both peppers to a medium-size mixing bowl. Stir to combine.

Pour the mixture into the prepared pan. Bake for 30 minutes, or until lightly browned on top. Serve with the tortilla chips for dipping.

YIELD: 12 SERVINGS

Kale & Artichoke Dip

*Coconut Oil * Kale * Greek Yogurt*

This is just like your favorite spinach and artichoke dip you'd get as an appetizer at a restaurant, but with healthier superfood substitutions such as kale and Greek yogurt. Super-easy to make and loved by all, it will probably be your new go-to party appetizer!

1 tablespoon (14 g) coconut oil

2 teaspoons minced garlic

2 cups (140 g) chopped, de-stemmed kale

½ cup (115 g) plain Greek yogurt

½ cup (50 g) grated Parmesan cheese

½ cup (60 g) shredded mozzarella cheese

½ cup (100 g) whipped cream cheese

1 (14-ounce, or 392 g) can artichoke hearts, drained and diced

¼ teaspoon sea salt

Pita chips, for serving

Preheat the oven to 325°F (170°C, or gas mark 3). Spray a 7½-inch (19-cm) pie pan with nonstick spray.

In a skillet over medium heat, melt the coconut oil. Add the garlic and kale, and sauté for approximately 5 minutes, until the kale is softened but not browned.

Add to a medium-size mixing bowl, then stir in the yogurt, cheeses, cream cheese, artichoke hearts, and salt. Scrape into the prepared baking dish.

Bake for 30 minutes, or until lightly browned and bubbling.

Serve with the pita chips.

YIELD: 6 SERVINGS

Walnut Hummus

* Chickpeas * Walnuts

Making your own hummus doesn't have to be hard or daunting. You just throw everything into a food processor and blend until smooth!

2 (15-ounce, or 420 g) cans chickpeas, rinsed and drained
Juice of 1 lemon
¼ cup (60 g) tahini
½ cup (60 g) walnuts
1 cup (140 g) pressed, cubed firm tofu
2 tablespoons (20 g) minced garlic
1 cup (235 ml) olive oil
1 teaspoon ground cumin
¼ teaspoon garlic powder
1 teaspoon sea salt
¼ teaspoon black pepper
Pita chips, for serving

Combine all the ingredients except the pita chips in a food processor. Blend until smooth. Serve with the chips.

YIELD: 2 CUPS (480 G)

7-Layer Greek Dip

⁎ Greek Yogurt ⁎ Quinoa ⁎ Chickpeas ⁎ Walnuts

I could eat this all day long: seven of my favorite ingredients stacked together into one fabulous dip! Your guests will not want to leave the snack table . . . ever.

FOR GREEK SAUCE:

¾ cup (172 g) plain Greek yogurt

¼ teaspoon sea salt

¼ teaspoon ground cumin

¼ teaspoon garlic powder

1 cup (120 g) peeled, seeded, and cubed cucumber

FOR LAYERED DIP:

1 cup (185 g) cooked quinoa

1 cup (240 g) Greek sauce (see above)

1 cup (180 g) diced roasted red pepper

1 cup (240 g) Walnut Hummus (opposite)

1 cup (100 g) diced black olives

1 cup (150 g) diced grape tomatoes

1 cup (150 g) crumbled feta cheese

Pita chips, for serving

To make the sauce: Combine the yogurt, salt, cumin, and garlic powder in a small bowl. Stir to combine. Add the cucumber and stir again.

To make the layered dip: In a medium-size serving bowl, layer the dip in the following order: quinoa on the bottom, Greek sauce, red pepper, hummus, olives, tomatoes, and feta on top. Serve with pita chips.

YIELD: 4 CUPS (920 G)

MAKE INDIVIDUAL CUPS

Try serving in small individual plastic cups for a party. There's less mess, and each party guest can have his or her very own and double-dip without judgment!

Fruit Skewers & Chocolate Coconut Dip

* *Greek Yogurt* * *Honey* * *Walnuts* * *Blueberries*

Impress your guests with these beautiful fruit skewers. The angel food cake dipped in dark chocolate and walnuts looks fancy, but these skewers are super easy to put together! If you don't have angel food cake, try using cubes of chocolate zucchini bread, doughnut holes, or any baked good of your choice that will hold its structural integrity when skewered and dipped.

FOR DIP:

¾ *cup (180 ml) coconut cream**

1½ *cups (345 g) plain Greek
  yogurt*

¼ *cup (80 g) honey*

2 *teaspoons pure vanilla extract*

2 *tablespoons (16 g) cocoa powder*

FOR SKEWERS:

¾ *cup (130 g) dark chocolate
  chips*

1½ *teaspoons vanilla almond milk*

¼ *angel food cake*

½ *cup (60 g) crushed walnuts*

½ *cup (75 g) fresh organic
  blueberries*

12 *strawberries, hulled*

12 *(6-inch, or 15-cm) wooden
  skewers*

** Refrigerate a 14-ounce (392 g)
can of coconut milk overnight. In
the morning, it will be separated
with one half of the can being pure
liquid and the other half being solid.
Discard the liquid and only use the
solid part for this recipe.*

To make the dip: Combine all the dip ingredients in a medium-size mixing bowl. Use a hand mixer to thoroughly blend until smooth.

To make the skewers: Melt the chocolate chips in a small saucepan over low heat. Add the almond milk and stir until smooth. Cut the angel food cake into square chunks. Spread the walnuts on a plate. Using a toothpick or extra skewer, dip the cake into the melted chocolate, then roll in the crushed walnuts.

Assemble your skewers by piercing the ingredients in this order: 2 blueberries, 1 chocolate-covered angel food cake piece, 2 blueberries, 1 strawberry, and 2 blueberries. Serve with the dip.

YIELD: 12 SKEWERS AND 2 CUPS (460 G) DIP

Southwestern Fiesta Dip

Need a last-minute party appetizer for that hungry crowd? This fabulous Southwestern dip can be put together in five minutes flat!

¾ *cup (172 g) plain Greek yogurt*

Juice of 1 lime

¼ *cup (32 g) dry ranch dressing mix*

½ *teaspoon sea salt*

½ *teaspoon cumin*

½ *cup (92 g) cooked quinoa, cooled*

½ *cup (120 g) black beans*

½ *cup (65 g) organic sweet corn kernels*

½ *cup (60 g) shredded Monterey Jack cheese*

½ *cup (75 g) diced grape tomatoes*

¼ *cup (38 g) diced red bell pepper*

1 *tablespoon (9 g) diced jalapeños*

Tortilla chips, for serving

Combine the yogurt, lime juice, ranch mix, salt, and cumin in a small bowl. Stir to blend.

In a separate bowl, combine the quinoa, beans, corn, cheese, tomatoes, bell pepper, and jalapeños. Stir to combine. Add the yogurt mixture and toss gently to mix.

Serve with the tortilla chips.

YIELD: 12 SERVINGS

Asian Sesame Dip

Why serve veggies to your guests with boring ranch dressing? This Asian Sesame Dip will add sophistication and flair, and it tastes delicious with all sorts of veggies and even wonton strips!

½ *cup (120 g) chickpeas, rinsed and drained*

2 *tablespoons (30 ml) sesame oil*

1½ *cups (345 g) plain Greek yogurt*

1 *tablespoon (8 g) white sesame seeds, toasted*

1 *tablespoon (15 ml) soy sauce*

1 *tablespoon (20 g) honey*

In a medium-size mixing bowl, puree the chickpeas and sesame oil with an immersion blender; a blender or food processor will also work.

Add the yogurt, sesame seeds, soy sauce, and honey to the mixture and stir to combine. Chill in the refrigerator for 1 hour before serving.

YIELD: 2 CUPS (460 G)

Sweet Potato Stacks

❋ *Sweet Potatoes* ❋ *Greek Yogurt*

Try adding other things to these sweet potato stacks, such as sweet kernel corn, roasted bell peppers, or black beans. They are the perfect size for a single bite. Put the whole thing in your mouth and enjoy the party!

2 sweet potatoes, sliced into rounds

¾ cup (172 g) plain Greek yogurt

Juice of ½ lime

A handful of cilantro leaves

4 slices turkey bacon, cooked and crumbled

1½ teaspoons paprika

Preheat the oven to 400°F (200°C, or gas mark 6). Spray a baking sheet with nonstick spray or line with foil or parchment paper.

Spread the sweet potato slices on a baking sheet in a single layer. Bake for 20 minutes, or until softened and slightly curled up around the edges.

Combine the Greek yogurt and lime juice in a small bowl.

Assemble the stacks in the following order: sweet potato slice, a dollop of yogurt sauce, a cilantro leaf (or two), a few crumbles of bacon, and a sprinkle of paprika.

YIELD: 24 TO 30 STACKS

Sweet Potato Tots with Creamy Ketchup

* Sweet Potatoes * Eggs * Greek Yogurt

Bring these sweet potato tots to your next party and you will be amazed at 1) how quickly they are devoured and 2) how many compliments you receive! Fry them earlier in the day, and then heat them up in the oven right before serving.

FOR TOTS:

1 large sweet potato, peeled

1 egg

¼ cup (30 g) unbleached all-purpose flour

¼ teaspoon sea salt

¼ teaspoon paprika

¼ teaspoon garlic powder

3 cups (705 ml) peanut oil, for deep-frying

FOR SAUCE:

¼ cup (58 g) plain Greek yogurt

¼ cup (60 g) ketchup

To make the tots: Bring a pot of water to a boil over high heat, add the sweet potato whole, and cook for approximately 15 minutes, until slightly softened, but not easily mashable with a fork, as you'll need to be able to grate it. Drain, let cool for 10 minutes, then shred with a cheese grater.

Add the shredded potato and egg to a medium-size bowl and stir with a fork to combine. In a separate bowl, whisk together the flour, salt, paprika, and garlic powder. Add to the potato mixture and stir to combine.

Pour the peanut oil into a deep fryer and heat it to 375°F (190°C) on an instant-read thermometer. Place a layer of paper towels on a plate for draining.

Form the mixture into 1-inch (2.5-cm) balls, then add in batches to the hot oil, being careful not to crowd the pot. Fry for 3 minutes. Remove with a spider or slotted spoon and drain on the paper towel–lined plate. Repeat with the remaining potato balls, bringing the oil back to temperature in between batches.

To make the sauce: Combine the yogurt and ketchup in a small bowl. Serve with the hot tots.

YIELD: 24 TO 36 TOTS

NO DEEP FRYER?

If you don't have a deep fryer, fry the tots in a deep-sided pan on the stove. Fill your pan with the oil and heat it for approximately 10 minutes over medium-high heat. Carefully add the tots and fry for 3 minutes, using a splatter screen to cover the pan.

Pad Thai Spring Rolls

* Chickpeas * Coconut Oil * Honey * Eggs

Traditional pad Thai toppings such as carrots, ham, cabbage, and eggs are stuffed into a soft spring roll wrapper, and then dipped into an amazing lime peanut sauce. Cut the rolls in half to serve to more party guests, or serve whole.

FOR SAUCE:

1 cup (285 g) Chickpea Nut Butter (page 29)

Juice of ½ lime

2 tablespoons (30 ml) soy sauce

1 tablespoon (14 g) coconut oil, melted

1 tablespoon (20 g) honey

FOR ROLLS:

1 tablespoon (14 g) coconut oil

6 eggs

12 rice paper skins

12 ounces (336 g) sliced smoked ham

4 carrots, spiralized or peeled into thin strips

1 head purple cabbage, shredded

To make the sauce: Combine all the sauce ingredients in a small mixing bowl.

To make the rolls: In a skillet over medium-low heat, melt the coconut oil. Crack in the eggs and add, stirring to scramble. Cook for 4 to 5 minutes, flipping halfway through, until the eggs are set. Remove from the skillet and slice into thin strips.

Fill a medium-size bowl with warm water, add the rice paper skins, and soak for 2 minutes to soften.

Lay out the rice paper skins on a work surface. Put 2 slices of ham, 3 strips of scrambled egg, a handful of carrot spirals, and a few strips of purple cabbage on each skin. Fold the top edge over, fold the sides in, and then finish rolling.

YIELD: 12 SPRING ROLLS

NO SPIRALIZER?

If you don't have a spiralizer or julienne peeler, you can use a regular handheld peeler to create thin strips of carrots for these rolls. Simply peel off the outer skin of the carrot (and discard those shavings), then continue to peel thin strips of carrots onto a plate.

Garlic-Roasted Kale Chips ➤

✹ Kale ✹ Coconut Oil

This is such an easy way to eat your greens! These kale chips are light, crispy, and made for garlic lovers. It looks like a lot of kale when you start, but it gets smaller after baking and it's hard not to eat the entire batch.

4 cups (280 g) de-stemmed kale, chopped into 2-inch (5-cm) pieces

1 tablespoon (14 g) coconut oil, melted

1 teaspoon garlic powder

¼ teaspoon sea salt

1 tablespoon (8 g) nutritional yeast

1 teaspoon minced garlic

Preheat the oven to 325°F (170°C, or gas mark 3). Spray a baking sheet with nonstick spray or line with parchment paper.

Combine all the ingredients in a large bowl, mixing thoroughly to make sure the kale leaves are evenly coated.

Spread the kale pieces flat on the prepared baking sheet, making sure they do not touch each other.

Bake for 15 minutes, then remove from the oven and let them cool for 10 minutes before eating.

YIELD: 2 SERVINGS

Pear, Walnut & Brie Crostini

✹ Coconut Oil ✹ Walnuts ✹ Honey

These elegant little crostini are bursting with flavor and scream sophistication. For a twist, put these toppings on a flatbread or pizza crust.

1 teaspoon coconut oil

1½ cups (240 g) cored and diced pears

¾ cup (90 g) chopped walnuts

¼ cup (80 g) honey, plus more for drizzling, if desired

1 teaspoon ground cinnamon

Sliced bread (I like sourdough)

12 ounces (336 g) Brie

Preheat the oven to 400°F (200°C, or gas mark 6).

Melt the oil in a skillet over medium heat. Stir in the pears, walnuts, honey, and cinnamon. Sauté for approximately 6 minutes, stirring to prevent sticking, until the pears are softened.

Spread the bread slices on a cookie sheet and bake for 10 minutes. Remove from the oven and top each slice of bread with a smear of Brie and a scoop of the pear mixture. Drizzle additional honey over the top.

YIELD: 18 TO 24 CROSTINI PIECES, DEPENDING ON THE BREAD

Walnut-Crusted Sea Scallops

* Walnuts * Eggs * Coconut Oil * Honey

There's just something so sophisticated about sea scallops. Maybe because they're slightly expensive and unique? Regardless, this is *the* way to prepare them. The walnut crust creates a fabulous crunch, and the sweet honey mustard sauce balances the nutty flavor perfectly.

FOR SCALLOPS:

12 ounces (336 g) wild sea scallops, fresh or frozen

½ cup (60 g) unbleached all-purpose flour

2 eggs, beaten

1 cup (120 g) coarsely chopped walnuts

2 tablespoons (28 g) coconut oil

FOR SAUCE:

2 tablespoons (22 g) yellow mustard

2 tablespoons (22 g) spicy brown mustard

¼ cup (80 g) honey

To make the scallops: If the sea scallops are frozen, defrost according to package directions.

Set out three small bowls: one with the flour, one with the eggs, and one with the walnuts.

Melt the coconut oil in a skillet over medium-high heat. Coat each sea scallop with the flour, then dip in the egg mixture, then coat with the crushed walnuts, pressing to adhere. Add to the hot skillet.

Cook for approximately 4 minutes on each side, flipping carefully with tongs to keep the coating intact. Scallops should be opaque white and not translucent when fully cooked.

To make the sauce: Combine the sauce ingredients in a small bowl. Dip the scallops in the sauce and enjoy!

YIELD: ABOUT 12 SCALLOPS

CHICKEN NUGGET ALTERNATIVE

If you don't like scallops, you're not alone. My husband is not the biggest fan (he thinks the seafood taste is too strong). So, I often make this recipe using small pieces of chicken instead. They're some of the best chicken nuggets we've ever had.

soups &
salads

Perfect for lunch, as a side dish, or even a full (lighter) dinner, these soups and salads are bright, colorful, and packed with nutrients. You will want to try each and every one and make them again and again.

Sweet Potato, Carrot & Apple Soup

* Coconut Oil * Sweet Potatoes * Chickpeas * Greek Yogurt

This is such a refreshing, light, and vitamin-rich soup, perfect for dinner or leftovers throughout the week. Try serving it with a dollop of Greek yogurt and toasted bread for dipping.

1 tablespoon (14 g) coconut oil

2 sweet potatoes, peeled and diced

1 tablespoon (8 g) minced garlic

3 apples, cored and diced (I like Fuji apples)

8 carrots, sliced

1 cup (240 g) chickpeas, rinsed and drained

4 cups (940 ml) chicken broth

11 ounces (310 ml) plain coconut water

1½ teaspoons ground ginger

1 teaspoon sea salt

2 tablespoons (5 g) minced fresh sage

2 cups (470 ml) water

Toasted bread, for serving

Greek yogurt, for serving (optional)

In a large stockpot over medium-high heat, melt the coconut oil. Add the sweet potatoes and garlic and sauté for approximately 5 minutes, until the sweet potatoes are softened. Add the apples, carrots, chickpeas, broth, coconut water, ginger, salt, sage, and water, bring to a boil, then lower the heat and simmer for 30 minutes, or until the carrots and apples are completely softened.

Using an immersion stick blender—a blender or food processor will also work—puree the soup until smooth. If using a blender, transfer the hot soup in batches and hold the lid of the blender with a pot holder.

Serve with the toasted bread and a dollop of Greek yogurt.

YIELD: 3 OR 4 SERVINGS

MAGICAL COCONUT WATER

Did you know that one 11-ounce (310 ml) serving of coconut water has more potassium than four bananas?! If you don't like drinking it plain, hide it in a fabulous soup recipe, such as the one above. It is a great addition to any broth-based soup.

Egg Drop Soup

✳ Coconut Oil ✳ Sweet Potatoes ✳ Eggs

Like takeout from your favorite Chinese restaurant but better, this egg drop soup is flavorful without being too thick or gelatinous. It's even quicker to put together than picking up takeout, too!

1½ teaspoons coconut oil
¼ cup (30 g) diced sweet potato
4 cups (940 ml) chicken broth
¼ teaspoon black pepper
¼ teaspoon ground ginger
½ teaspoon garlic powder
1½ teaspoons sesame oil
1½ teaspoons soy sauce
½ cup (65 g) sweet corn kernels,
   rinsed and drained
1 tablespoon (6 g) diced scallion
4 eggs, lightly beaten
2½ tablespoons (20 g) cornstarch

Melt the coconut oil in a skillet over medium-high heat. Sauté the sweet potato for approximately 5 minutes, until softened.

In a stockpot, combine the chicken broth, black pepper, ginger, garlic powder, sesame oil, soy sauce, corn, and sweet potato. Heat to a slow boil, approximately 10 minutes.

Add the eggs, slowly stirring with a whisk to make the pieces form strands.

In a small bowl, combine a ladleful of the broth with the cornstarch, stirring to remove any lumps. Whisk into the soup (it should thicken slightly). Remove from the heat and serve hot.

YIELD: 3 SERVINGS

Ham & White Bean Soup

∗ Coconut Oil ∗ Kale ∗ Honey ∗ Chickpeas

This hearty, flavorful soup is my husband's favorite way to eat chickpeas! I think it's because they blend in so well with the ham. With a full cup of kale per serving, getting your greens has never been so easy. If you can't find the Montreal steak seasoning, substitute 1 teaspoon sea salt and 1 teaspoon black pepper.

1 tablespoon (14 g) coconut oil

3 cups (450 g) diced, cooked ham

4 cups (280 g) diced, de-stemmed kale

1 tablespoon (8 g) minced garlic

¼ cup (65 g) barbecue sauce

1 tablespoon (15 ml) Worcestershire sauce

1 tablespoon (15 g) ketchup

1 tablespoon (20 g) honey

1 tablespoon (8 g) Montreal steak seasoning

4 cups (940 ml) chicken broth

4 cups (940 ml) water

2 (15-ounce, or 420 g) cans chickpeas, rinsed and drained

In a large stockpot over medium-high heat, melt the coconut oil. Add the ham, kale, and garlic. Simmer for approximately 5 minutes, stirring frequently, until the kale is softened and the garlic is lightly browned (being careful not to burn).

Add the barbecue sauce, Worcestershire sauce, ketchup, honey, steak seasoning, broth, water, and chickpeas, lower the heat to medium, and simmer for an additional 30 minutes. Serve hot.

YIELD: 4 SERVINGS

Coconut Curried Soup

❋ Coconut Oil ❋ Chickpeas ❋ Greek Yogurt ❋ Quinoa

Don't let the curry or bright yellow color scare you. This soup has a nice mild flavor, enriched by the chickpeas and quinoa. And besides, curry powder is good for you! It helps regulate blood sugar and lower bad cholesterol.

1 tablespoon (14 g) coconut oil

¾ cup (98 g) thinly sliced carrot

1 teaspoon minced garlic

4 cups (940 ml) chicken broth

1 (14-ounce, or 392 g) can coconut milk

2 (15-ounce, or 420 g) cans chickpeas, rinsed and drained

1 tablespoon (6 g) yellow curry powder

¼ teaspoon ground turmeric

¼ teaspoon ground ginger

¼ teaspoon black pepper

½ cup (115 g) plain Greek yogurt

1 cup (185 g) cooked quinoa

In a stockpot over medium-high heat, melt the coconut oil. Add the carrots and garlic and sauté for approximately 5 minutes, until lightly browned.

Add the broth, coconut milk, chickpeas, curry powder, turmeric, ginger, pepper, yogurt, and quinoa and stir to combine. Heat to a slow boil, reduce the heat to medium, and simmer for 30 minutes, or until the chickpeas are soft. Serve hot.

YIELD: 4 TO 6 SERVINGS

CHICKEN VERSION

If you feel a meal is not complete without meat (or someone in your family feels this way), try adding shredded chicken. It blends seamlessly with the flavors of this soup.

Creamy Chicken Corn Chowder

*** Coconut Oil * Eggs***

The ultimate comfort food, this creamy, meat-filled soup is über filling yet lightened up with coconut water and chicken broth instead of heavy cream. Feel free to add cubed Yukon gold potatoes if you want to bulk up the soup even more.

1 boneless, skinless chicken breast

2 tablespoons (28 g) coconut oil

¼ white onion, diced

1 orange bell pepper, cored and diced

2 cups (260 g) sweet corn kernels, rinsed and drained

2 cups (470 ml) chicken broth

1½ cups (355 ml) plain coconut water

2 cups (470 ml) milk

½ cup (60 g) shredded Cheddar cheese

4 slices turkey bacon, cooked and crumbled

1 teaspoon garlic powder

½ teaspoon ground cumin

½ teaspoon sea salt

2 egg yolks

2 tablespoons (16 g) flour

Place a medium pot of water over high heat and bring to a boil. Add the chicken breast, and cook for 10 minutes, or until cooked through. Remove the chicken from the water and let cool for 10 minutes before shredding with a fork or by hand.

In a stockpot over medium-high heat, melt the coconut oil. Add the onion, bell pepper, and corn and sauté for approximately 5 minutes, until lightly browned.

Add the chicken, broth, coconut water, milk, cheese, bacon, garlic powder, cumin, and salt. Stir to combine. Heat to a slow boil, then let simmer for 20 minutes.

Whisk in the egg yolks and flour, making sure no lumps of flour are visible. Let cook for an additional 5 minutes, then remove from the heat and serve hot.

YIELD: 4 SERVINGS

Sweet Potato Chickpea Chili with Quinoa

* Coconut Oil * Sweet Potatoes * Chickpeas * Honey * Quinoa

My husband saw me create this recipe and, seeing the ingredients, was initially not enthused. However, he was so enamored by the smell in our kitchen that he insisted on trying it . . . and loved it!!

2 tablespoons (28 g) coconut oil

4 cups (440 g) peeled and diced sweet potatoes

½ cup (80 g) diced white onion

1 (15-ounce, or 420 g) can diced tomatoes, not drained

4 cups (940 ml) chicken broth

2 (15-ounce, or 420 g) cans chickpeas, rinsed and drained

1 cup (235 ml) water

1 cup (235 ml) apple cider

2 tablespoons (15 g) chili powder

1 tablespoon (20 g) honey

1 tablespoon (20 g) molasses

½ teaspoon dry mustard

½ teaspoon sea salt

½ teaspoon ground cumin

1 cup (185 g) cooked quinoa

In a large stockpot over medium-high heat, melt the coconut oil. Add the sweet potatoes and onion and sauté for approximately 8 minutes, until softened. Add the tomatoes, broth, chickpeas, water, apple cider, chili powder, honey, molasses, dry mustard, salt, cumin, and quinoa. Stir to combine.

Simmer on medium-high heat for 20 minutes, stirring occasionally to prevent sticking. Reduce the heat to low and simmer for another 40 minutes, or until the sweet potatoes and chickpeas are soft.

YIELD: 4 SERVINGS

MEAT LOVERS VERSION

Not convinced a vegetarian sweet potato chili will appeal to your meat-loving family? Feel free to add ½ cup (112 g) browned ground beef.

Italian Wedding Soup with Balsamic Blueberry Chicken Meatballs

* Blueberries * Kale * Chickpeas

Classic Italian wedding soup gets a modern twist with beautiful balsamic blueberry meatballs. I know they sound unusual, but they taste divine! Embrace your adventurous side in the kitchen, and try them at least once.

FOR MEATBALLS:

1½ cups (75 g) cubed sourdough bread (crusts removed)

1 cup (225 g) ground chicken or beef

¼ cup (25 g) grated Parmesan cheese

1 teaspoon each white balsamic vinegar, sea salt, and dried basil

½ teaspoon black pepper

½ cup (75 g) fresh organic blueberries

3 cups (705 ml) vegetable oil, for frying

FOR SOUP:

¾ cup (98 g) diced carrots

1½ cups (105 g) diced, de-stemmed kale

8 cups (1880 ml) chicken broth

1 teaspoon each dried oregano, dried basil, and minced garlic

1 (15-ounce, or 420 g) can crushed tomatoes

1¼ cups (300 g) chickpeas, rinsed and drained

½ cup (50 g) grated Parmesan cheese

Sliced sourdough bread, for serving (optional)

Grated Parmesan cheese, for serving (optional)

To make the meatballs: Combine the bread cubes, chicken, cheese, vinegar, salt, basil, and pepper in a medium mixing bowl. Mix thoroughly with your hands—the bread cubes should fall apart somewhat to combine with the meat. Add the blueberries and mix gently to combine.

Pour the vegetable oil into a deep fryer and heat it to 375°F (190°C) on an instant-read thermometer. Place a layer of paper towels on a plate for draining.

Form the meatballs into approximately ¾-inch (2-cm) balls, then carefully add in batches to the hot oil, being careful not to crowd the pot, and fry for 2 minutes. Remove with a spider or slotted spoon and drain on the paper towel–lined plate. Repeat with the remaining meatballs, bringing the oil back to temperature in between batches.

To make the soup: In a large stockpot over high heat, combine all the soup ingredients. Bring to a boil, then simmer over medium-high heat for approximately 20 minutes, or until the carrots, kale, and chickpeas are soft. Add the meatballs and simmer for an additional 10 minutes.

If serving with the bread and cheese, preheat the broiler. Sprinkle the sourdough bread with the Parmesan. Place on a baking sheet and heat under the broiler until the cheese is melted, 2 to 3 minutes. Serve with the soup.

YIELD: 4 SERVINGS

Salmon Chowder with Cashew Cream

★ Coconut Oil ★ Sweet Potatoes

I really can't say enough good things about this soup. It is absolutely perfect. Savory, scrumptious, and full of nourishing ingredients, it's also dairy-free because it uses "cashew cream" instead of traditional half-and-half.

2 cups (240 g) raw cashews

2 cups (470 ml) water, divided

1 tablespoon (14 g) coconut oil

2 carrots, thinly sliced

½ sweet onion, diced

1 sweet potato, peeled and diced

2 tablespoons (16 g) minced garlic

2 tablespoons (8 g) chopped fresh parsley

8 cups (1880 ml) chicken broth

¼ cup (32 g) nutritional yeast flakes

12 ounces (336 g) frozen wild-caught salmon, thawed

Bread, for serving

In a medium-size bowl, soak the cashews in 1 cup (235 ml) of the water for 3 hours. Drain the water and add the remaining 1 cup (235 ml) water to the cashews. Puree with an immersion blender, food processor, or blender, and then set aside. This is your cashew cream.

In a large stockpot over medium-high heat, melt the coconut oil. Add the carrots, onion, sweet potato, and garlic and sauté for approximately 5 minutes, or until the onion is softened and slightly browned.

Add the parsley, broth, cashew cream, and nutritional yeast and stir to combine. Bring the mixture to a boil, then reduce the heat to medium and simmer for approximately 15 minutes, until the sweet potatoes are softened and the soup is at a slow, rolling boil.

Add the wild salmon. The boiling soup will cook the salmon in about 8 minutes. Once the salmon is cooked through, use a fork to flake it into small pieces. Serve with bread for dipping.

YIELD: 4 SERVINGS

GIVE CASHEW CREAM A TRY

Even if you're not dairy-free, this cashew cream is definitely worth trying! It has a fabulous nutty flavor in addition to its creaminess and heart-healthy fats. My toddler ate an entire bowl of this chowder without any fussing (or prodding by me)!

Tuscan Kale Soup

* Coconut Oil ✳ Kale ✳ Quinoa

This hearty Italian soup is packed with protein and more than a full day's worth of vitamins C, A, and K! On its own or served with a provolone and Parmesan grilled cheese sandwich, this meal is sure to please everyone at the table.

FOR SOUP:

2 boneless, skinless chicken breasts

1 tablespoon (14 g) coconut oil

1 tablespoon (15 ml) olive oil

2 tablespoons (20 g) diced white onion

4 cups (280 g) diced, de-stemmed kale

1 tablespoon (8 g) minced garlic

4 cups (940 ml) chicken broth

4 cups (940 ml) water

2 tablespoons (30 ml) white balsamic vinegar

1 teaspoon sea salt

1 teaspoon dried oregano

1 teaspoon dried basil

2 cups (300 g) halved grape tomatoes

1½ cups (278 g) cooked quinoa

FOR EACH SANDWICH:

2 slices sandwich bread

1 teaspoon unsalted butter

1 slice provolone cheese

⅓ cup (35 g) grated Parmesan cheese

To make the soup: Bring the water in a medium pot to a boil over high heat, add the chicken breast, and cook for 10 minutes, or until cooked through. Remove the chicken from the water and let cool for 10 minutes before shredding with a fork or by hand.

In a large stockpot over medium heat, melt the coconut oil, and then add the olive oil, onion, kale, and garlic. Sauté for approximately 6 minutes, until the onion is slightly browned. Add the shredded chicken, broth, water, vinegar, salt, oregano, basil, tomatoes, and quinoa. Stir to combine. Simmer for 30 minutes, to soften the kale and let the flavors meld.

To make the sandwich: Spread the butter on the outside of each slice of bread. Place one slice of bread, buttered side down, in a medium skillet, place the provolone cheese on top, spread the Parmesan over the cheese, then top with the other slice of bread, buttered side up. Cook over medium heat for about 6 minutes, flipping halfway through, until the bread is browned on both sides and the cheese is melted. Serve with the soup.

YIELD: 3 OR 4 SERVINGS

Chinese Chopped Salad with Orange Sesame Dressing

* Honey * Kale

A lot of people are scared of kale salad, afraid that it just won't taste very good. But you don't have to be scared! This salad is fabulous with the citrus taking away any hint of bitterness. The other plus to kale salad is that it makes great leftovers because it doesn't wilt like traditional (dressed) lettuce does.

FOR SALAD:

1 thick slice (round) red onion

1 tablespoon (20 g) honey

8 cups (560 g) diced, de-stemmed kale

¼ cup (60 ml) sesame oil

1 orange, peeled and separated into slices

¼ cup (35 g) cashews

1 tablespoon (8 g) white sesame seeds, toasted

½ orange bell pepper, cored and diced

FOR DRESSING:

¼ cup (60 ml) clementine juice

1 tablespoon (15 ml) rice vinegar

1 tablespoon (20 g) honey

1 tablespoon (15 ml) sesame oil

⅛ teaspoon ground ginger

1½ teaspoons cornstarch

To make the salad: In a skillet over medium heat, sauté the onion with the honey for approximately 8 minutes, flipping halfway through. The rings do not need to stay intact. However, you want the onions to caramelize and get slightly brown, but not burn.

Combine the kale and sesame oil in a large mixing bowl. Gently massage the oil into the kale leaves by hand for approximately 2 minutes. This helps reduce the bitterness and softens the texture of the kale. Add the sautéed onion, orange, cashews, sesame seeds, and bell pepper and toss to combine.

To make the dressing: In a separate bowl, combine all the dressing ingredients and whisk to blend.

Pour the dressing over the salad (you may not need all of it) and mix thoroughly.

YIELD: 3 OR 4 SERVINGS

Berry & Quinoa Salad with Goat Cheese

Quinoa ✳ *Blueberries* ✳ *Walnuts* ✳ *Honey*

The goat cheese adds a wonderful creaminess and balances the sweet berries in this summer salad. It's perfect as a side dish or on its own. You can also try substituting plain Greek yogurt if you don't have any goat cheese on hand.

2 cups (370 g) cooked quinoa, cooled

½ cup (60 g) coarsely chopped walnuts

2 cups (340 g) hulled and sliced strawberries

1 cup (150 g) fresh organic blueberries

2 tablespoons (40 g) honey

1 cup (150 g) crumbled goat cheese

Combine the quinoa and walnuts in a medium-size mixing bowl. Stir thoroughly. Gently fold in the strawberries and blueberries. Drizzle with the honey, add the goat cheese, and toss to combine. Serve cold.

YIELD: 4 SERVINGS

UNSURE ABOUT GOAT CHEESE?

If you are unsure about whether your child (or you!) will like goat cheese, try substituting a milder cheese such as Havarti. Or omit the cheese altogether.

Chopped Purple Power Salad

* Kale * Quinoa * Walnuts * Chickpeas * Honey * Greek Yogurt

I would like to rename this salad "The Miracle Salad." Why? Because not only is it packed with six of the ten superfoods, but Babycakes (my 4-year-old) declared this to be her new "most favorite food EVER" and devoured three bowls of it. Move over PB&J, there's a new favorite in town!

FOR SALAD:

2 tablespoons (30 ml) sesame oil

1 cup (70 g) diced, de-stemmed kale

¾ head purple cabbage, shredded and diced (approximately 3 cups [270 g])

1 cup (185 g) cooked quinoa

¾ cup (90 g) coarsely chopped walnuts

¼ cup (38 g) crumbled goat cheese

FOR DRESSING:

¼ cup (60 g) chickpeas, rinsed and drained

1 tablespoon (15 ml) soy sauce

2 tablespoons (40 g) honey

1 tablespoon (15 g) plain Greek yogurt

To make the salad: Combine the sesame oil and kale in a large mixing bowl. Gently massage the oil into the kale leaves by hand for approximately 2 minutes. This helps reduce the bitterness and softens the texture of the kale. Add the cabbage, quinoa, walnuts, and goat cheese and toss gently to combine.

To make the dressing: In a separate bowl, combine all the dressing ingredients in a bowl and use an immersion blender—a food processor or blender will also work—to puree until smooth.

Pour the dressing over the salad and toss thoroughly to combine.

YIELD: 3 OR 4 SERVINGS

Quinoa, Grapefruit & Golden Beet Salad

* Kale * Coconut Oil * Quinoa * Honey

Roasting the pears, golden beets, and grapefruit really brings out the flavor and complements the kale and quinoa so nicely. As for the dressing, I'd like to drink it with a straw it's so yummy!

FOR SALAD:

1 golden beet, peeled and sliced

1 pear, peeled and cubed

1 grapefruit, peeled, sectioned, and inner skins removed

1 teaspoon olive oil

1 teaspoon sea salt

1 tablespoon (14 g) coconut oil, melted

4 cups (280 g) diced, de-stemmed kale

3 cups (555 g) cooked quinoa

FOR DRESSING:

¼ cup (60 ml) freshly squeezed grapefruit juice

2 tablespoons (30 ml) apple cider vinegar

1 tablespoon (20 g) molasses

1 tablespoon (20 g) honey

2 teaspoons minced garlic

To make the salad: Preheat the oven to 400°F (200°C, or gas mark 6).

Spread the beet slices, pear cubes, and grapefruit sections in a single layer on a baking sheet. Drizzle with the olive oil and then sprinkle with the sea salt. Toss to coat. Bake for 20 minutes, or until lightly browned. Let cool on the baking sheet.

Combine the coconut oil and kale in a large mixing bowl. Gently massage the oil into the kale leaves by hand for approximately 2 minutes. This helps reduce the bitterness and softens the texture of the kale. Add the beets, pears, grapefruit, and quinoa and toss gently to combine.

To make the dressing: Combine the dressing ingredients in a small bowl. Pour over the salad, toss to coat, and enjoy!

YIELD: 4 SERVINGS

PREPARING GRAPEFRUIT

To prepare the grapefruit for roasting, first remove the thick outer peel. Break the grapefruit apart into sections. With a sharp paring knife, cut open each individual section to remove the thinner (inner) skin as well. All that should remain is the brightly colored grapefruit flesh.

Salmon Spinach Salad with Creamy Yogurt Dressing

✶ Coconut Oil ✶ Walnuts ✶ Eggs ✶ Greek Yogurt ✶ Honey

This salad is hearty enough for lunch or even dinner. The creamy dressing is so delicious with the baked salmon. Don't tell anyone, but you could even forget the spinach salad and just eat the salmon and sauce!

FOR DRESSING:

¾ cup (172 g) plain Greek yogurt

1 tablespoon (20 g) honey

1 tablespoon (15 ml) sesame oil

1 teaspoon minced garlic

FOR SALAD:

2 (8-ounce, or 224 g) pieces frozen wild-caught salmon

1 tablespoon (14 g) coconut oil, melted

2 teaspoons minced garlic

8 cups (240 g) baby spinach

1 cup (150 g) diced orange bell pepper

1 cup (120 g) coarsely chopped walnuts

4 hard-boiled eggs, peeled and sliced

Preheat the oven to 400°F (200°C, or gas mark 6).

To make the dressing: Combine the dressing ingredients in a small bowl and stir well.

To make the salad: Place the frozen salmon in a baking dish and pour the coconut oil over it. Rub the minced garlic on top. Bake for 25 minutes, or until the fish is opaque and cooked through. Slice and divide into 4 equal portions.

Assemble each salad with 2 cups (60 g) of the baby spinach, ¼ cup (37 g) of the diced bell pepper, ¼ cup (30 g) of the chopped walnuts, one-fourth of the cooked salmon slices, 1 hard-boiled egg, and ¼ cup (60 ml) of the yogurt dressing.

YIELD: 4 SERVINGS

Honey Mustard Chicken Salad

✻ Honey ✻ Greek Yogurt

Making my own salad dressing always seemed really daunting and something only my mother would do. But, let me assure you, it is so easy (and delicious)! This dressing is the perfect accompaniment to any summer salad.

FOR SALAD:

4 cups (220 g) mixed greens

½ cup (75 g) pitted and diced Rainier cherries

¾ cup (105 g) cooked and shredded chicken

¼ cup (30 g) shredded mozzarella cheese

FOR DRESSING:

¼ cup (60 ml) olive oil

2 tablespoons (40 g) honey

2 tablespoons (30 ml) apple cider vinegar

3 tablespoons (45 g) plain Greek yogurt

1 tablespoon (11 g) spicy brown mustard

½ teaspoon sea salt

To make the salad: Add the salad ingredients to a large mixing bowl and toss to combine.

To make the dressing: Combine the dressing ingredients in a large measuring cup and stir thoroughly. Serve the salad with the dressing on the side.

YIELD: 4 SERVINGS

Mexican Spinach Salad with Avocado Lime Vinaigrette

✳ Coconut Oil ✳ Honey

This is such a simple salad, but one I make over and over again. The creamy avocado lime dressing totally makes this dish! It's like a fiesta on a plate.

FOR SALAD:

4 cups (120 g) baby spinach

½ cup (120 g) black beans

¼ cup (30 g) shredded Cheddar cheese

½ cup (65 g) sweet corn kernels, rinsed and drained

2 tablespoons (2 g) chopped cilantro

FOR VINAIGRETTE:

2 tablespoons (28 g) coconut oil, melted

2 tablespoons (40 g) honey

2 tablespoons (30 ml) apple cider vinegar

2 tablespoons (30 ml) fresh lime juice

2 tablespoons (20 g) mashed avocado

To make the salad: Combine the salad ingredients in a large mixing bowl.

To make the vinaigrette: Combine the ingredients in a large measuring cup. Use an immersion blender—a blender or food processor will also work—to puree until smooth.

Serve the salad with the dressing on the side.

YIELD: 4 SERVINGS

Honeydew Caprese Salad with Quinoa

❋ Coconut Oil ❋ Quinoa

Honeydew has found its true calling in life. I typically do not enjoy honeydew melon on its own (give me watermelon or cantaloupe instead, please), but it is the perfect addition to this Caprese salad! Each bite is juicy and mouthwatering, a perfect blend of sweet and tangy.

¼ cup (56 g) coconut oil, melted

¼ cup (60 ml) white balsamic vinegar

2 tablespoons (16 g) minced garlic

1 tablespoon (15 g) basil paste or 20 fresh basil leaves

3 cups (450 g) diced grape tomatoes

1 cup (170 g) diced honeydew melon

1 cup (185 g) cooked red quinoa, cooled

1 pound (454 g) fresh mozzarella, cubed

Salt and pepper, to taste

Combine the oil, vinegar, garlic, and basil paste in a small bowl (if using basil leaves, add at the next step). Whisk to blend.

In a medium-size mixing bowl, combine the tomatoes, melon, quinoa, and mozzarella. Toss gently to combine. Pour the dressing over the salad, toss gently to coat, and season with salt and pepper. Serve cold.

YIELD: 6 SERVINGS

Creamy Pasta Salad with Bacon

＊ Greek Yogurt ＊ Honey

The great thing about pasta salad is that it makes a lot, doesn't cost all that much, and party guests love it! It's the perfect side dish to accompany burgers on the grill, deli sandwiches, or leafy green salads.

1½ cups (150 g) medium-size pasta shells

¾ cup (52 g) chopped broccoli

1 cup (130 g) fresh or frozen peas, defrosted if needed

½ cup (65 g) thinly sliced carrot

6 slices turkey bacon, cooked and crumbled

1 cup (120 g) grated Cheddar cheese

1 cup (230 g) plain Greek yogurt

1 tablespoon (20 g) honey

2 tablespoons (16 g) dry ranch dressing mix

Bring a pot of salted water to a boil over high heat, add the pasta, and cook according to the package directions. Remove the pasta with a slotted spoon, drain in a colander, and let cool for 10 minutes.

Return the pot of water to a boil. Add the broccoli and blanch for 1 minute. Drain and let cool.

Combine the cooled pasta, broccoli, peas, carrot, bacon, and cheese in a large mixing bowl.

In a small bowl, combine the yogurt, honey, and ranch mix and whisk to blend. Pour over the salad and toss gently to coat. Serve cold.

YIELD: 8 SERVINGS

sandwiches &
quesadillas

From pad Thai to pesto to smashed berry grilled cheese, these sandwiches, quesadillas, and wraps are big on flavor. They're perfect to pack for lunch at the office, a summer picnic, or a quick bite at home.

Smashed Berry & Balsamic Kale Grilled Cheese

✳ Coconut Oil ✳ Kale ✳ Blueberries

I confess, this might be my favorite recipe in the entire cookbook! The combination of flavors is over-the-top amazing. This is the only way to make grilled cheese from this day forward.

2 teaspoons coconut oil

1 cup (70 g) finely diced, de-stemmed kale

2 teaspoons balsamic vinegar

2 teaspoons basil paste or 10 fresh basil leaves

1 cup (150 g) organic blueberries

½ cup (75 g) organic blackberries

12 ounces (336 g) fontina cheese, sliced

8 slices sourdough bread

Preheat the oven to 375°F (190°C, or gas mark 5). In a medium-size skillet over medium heat, melt the coconut oil. Add the kale and sauté for approximately 5 minutes, until softened, and then add the balsamic vinegar and basil paste and stir to combine. Remove from the heat.

Smash the berries in a medium-size bowl. (I use the bottom of a cup to smash mine.)

For each sandwich, place a slice of sourdough bread, a layer of the kale mixture, a layer of sliced fontina cheese, and a layer of smashed berries, and then top with the second slice of bread. Set the sandwiches on a cookie sheet and bake in the oven for 10 minutes, or until the cheese is thoroughly melted. Serve hot.

YIELD: 4 SANDWICHES

BERRY SWAP

Feel free to substitute the berries for whatever kind is readily available or on sale. My husband doesn't like the texture of blackberries because of the tiny seeds inside. So, I substituted strawberries in his grilled cheese. It was absolutely delicious!

Turkey, Cranberry & Sweet Potato Stack

❋ Sweet Potatoes ❋ Quinoa ❋ Honey

Even though these are traditional Thanksgiving flavors, this sandwich should be enjoyed year-round. The combination of textures with the crunchy bacon, smooth cranberry sauce, and creamy goat cheese can't be beat!

1 sweet potato, baked and flesh scooped out

½ cup (92 g) cooked quinoa

1 tablespoon (20 g) honey

½ teaspoon ground cinnamon

4 slices bread

12 slices roast turkey

6 slices turkey bacon

½ (14-ounce, or 392 g) can cranberry sauce, cut into 4 slices

2 tablespoons (18 g) crumbled goat cheese or shredded Havarti

Combine the sweet potato flesh, quinoa, honey, and cinnamon in a small bowl, stirring and mashing well.

For each sandwich, spread a thick layer of the sweet potato mixture on 1 slice of bread. Top with 6 slices of the turkey, 3 slices of the bacon, 2 slices of the cranberry sauce, 1 tablespoon (9 g) of the goat cheese, and the second slice of bread.

YIELD: 2 SANDWICHES

Sweet Potato, Walnut & Havarti Grilled Cheese

This is like sweet potato casserole in grilled cheese form, except without the overly sugary marshmallows. You will want to devour it just the same, though!

1 large sweet potato, baked and flesh scooped out

1 teaspoon ground cinnamon

1 tablespoon (20 g) honey

⅓ cup (40 g) coarsely chopped walnuts

8 slices sourdough bread

16 slices Havarti cheese

Preheat the oven to 350°F (180°C, or gas mark 4).

In a small bowl, combine the sweet potato flesh, cinnamon, honey, and walnuts. Mash and stir to combine.

For each sandwich, spread 1 piece of bread with a thick layer of the sweet potato mixture, 4 slices of Havarti, and the second piece of bread. Place on a cookie sheet and bake for 10 minutes, until the cheese is melted and the bread is lightly browned.

YIELD: 4 SANDWICHES

Turkey, Caramelized Onion & Sautéed Pear Sammie

✷ Honey ✷ Chickpeas

Everything that might normally be on a delicious spinach salad is transformed into a one-of-a-kind sandwich in this recipe. The sweet pears and caramelized onions are balanced out by the garlicky hummus and spinach. And the best news? This sandwich is great hours later!

8 round slices yellow onion
½ teaspoon baking soda
2 teaspoons honey
1 pear, sliced (not peeled)
8 slices bread
½ cup (112 g) garlic hummus
1 pound (454 g) roasted turkey
32 spinach leaves

In a medium-size skillet over medium heat, add the onion slices, then sprinkle on the baking soda and drizzle on the honey. Sauté for approximately 4 minutes on each side, until the onions are softened, lightly browned, and starting to caramelize. Remove the onions from the skillet.

Add the sliced pears to the already hot skillet. Sauté for approximately 5 minutes, until the pears are softened and lightly browned.

For each sandwich, spread 1 slice of bread with 2 tablespoons (28 g) of the hummus, and then top with 2 slices of caramelized onions, a couple of pear slices, 5 or 6 slices of turkey, 8 spinach leaves, and the second slice of bread.

YIELD: 4 SANDWICHES

Blueberry & Walnut Chicken Salad Sandwich

* Blueberries * Walnuts * Greek Yogurt * Honey

This is one of my favorite sandwiches! The dried blueberries are a nice spin on the raisins and grapes used in traditional chicken salads, and the diced cucumber gives it a light refreshing taste.

2 boneless, skinless chicken breasts

½ cup (75 g) dried organic blueberries

½ cup (60 g) diced cucumber

½ cup (60 g) chopped walnuts

¾ cup (172 g) plain Greek yogurt

2 teaspoons honey

1 teaspoon pure vanilla extract

½ teaspoon ground cumin

½ teaspoon sea salt

4 croissants, split lengthwise

Bring water in a medium pot to a boil over high heat, add the chicken breast, and cook for 10 minutes, or until cooked through. Remove the chicken from the water and let cool for 10 minutes before shredding with a fork or by hand.

Combine the chicken, blueberries, cucumber, walnuts, yogurt, honey, vanilla, cumin, and salt in a medium-size mixing bowl. Stir thoroughly.

Divide the mixture evenly among the croissants and serve.

YIELD: 4 SANDWICHES

FRESH VS. DRIED

You can substitute fresh blueberries for the dried ones called for in this recipe if you need to. However, I like the texture and sweetness of the dried ones best. They act more like a raisin or dried cherry that you'd typically find in a chicken salad.

⤆ Pad Thai Sandwich

* Chickpeas * Coconut Oil * Honey * Eggs

Why have I never thought of this combination before?! I love peanut sauce. I love eggs. I love pad Thai. Soooooo, I combined them all into one fabulous, mouthwatering sandwich.

½ cup (142 g) *Chickpea Nut Butter (page 29)*

Juice of ½ lime

1½ teaspoons soy sauce

½ teaspoon coconut oil

2 eggs

4 slices bread, toasted

12 slices smoked ham

1 cup (130 g) grated carrot

Combine the Chickpea Nut Butter, lime juice, and soy sauce in a small bowl.

In a medium-size skillet over medium-high heat, melt the coconut oil. Add the eggs, making sure not to let them touch. Do not stir. Cover the skillet with a glass lid and let cook for 3 minutes. The yolk should not be too runny.

For each sandwich, smear the chickpea sauce on 1 slice of the toasted bread. Top with 6 slices of the ham, half of the grated carrot, 1 fried egg, and the second slice of bread. Dig in.

YIELD: 2 SANDWICHES

Egg Salad Sandwich

* Eggs * Greek Yogurt

Ditch the mayonnaise: permanently. You won't miss it when you taste this fabulous Greek yogurt–based egg salad! I love toasting the bread for a little crunch to balance the soft egg salad.

6 hard-boiled eggs, peeled and diced

⅓ cup (75 g) Greek yogurt

2 tablespoons (30 g) sweet pickle relish

Salt and pepper, to taste

6 slices bread, lightly toasted

Combine the diced eggs, Greek yogurt, and sweet relish in a medium-size mixing bowl. Season with salt and pepper.

For each sandwich, spread one-third of the egg salad on 1 slice of bread, then top with the second slice of bread.

YIELD: 3 SANDWICHES

Sunset Sliders

* Chickpeas * Quinoa * Walnuts * Eggs * Coconut Oil * Greek Yogurt

These Indian-inspired sliders are light, veggie-packed, and delicious! Be sure to top your slider with a generous dollop of the tangy Greek yogurt sauce.

FOR SLIDERS:

6 carrots, peeled

1 (15-ounce, or 420 g) can chickpeas, rinsed and drained

½ cup (92 g) cooked quinoa

½ cup (60 g) chopped walnuts

1 egg

½ orange bell pepper, cored and diced

½ cup (60 g) unbleached all-purpose flour

1 teaspoon ground curry

½ teaspoon sea salt

1 teaspoon minced garlic

2 teaspoons spicy brown mustard

FOR SAUCE:

¾ cup (172 g) plain Greek yogurt

1 teaspoon lemon juice

1 teaspoon curry

1 tablespoon (14 g) coconut oil

12 slider buns

To make the sliders: Combine the carrots, chickpeas, quinoa, walnuts, egg, bell pepper, flour, curry, salt, garlic, and mustard in a food processor. Blend until thoroughly combined. Refrigerate for 1 hour.

To make the sauce: Combine the sauce ingredients in a small bowl. Refrigerate until ready to serve.

Remove the slider mixture from the refrigerator and form into twelve 2-inch (5-cm) patties.

In a medium-size skillet over medium-high heat, melt the coconut oil. Pan-fry the slider patties in batches for 8 minutes on one side, then flip and cook for an additional 6 minutes. Both sides should be golden brown.

Serve on a slider bun with the yogurt sauce.

YIELD: 12 SLIDERS

Chickpea Pesto Bagelwich

✳ Chickpeas ✳ Greek Yogurt

So filling, so creamy, and so protein-packed, this sandwich will curb your hunger for the entire afternoon! This is a weekly staple at our house. Try adding sliced tomatoes or roasted turkey to change things up. Or serve it in a bowl with pita crisps.

FOR PESTO FILLING:

1 (15-ounce, or 420 g) can chickpeas, rinsed and drained

1 cup (225 g) diced avocado

¼ cup (60 g) Greek yogurt

2 tablespoons (30 g) basil paste or 40 fresh basil leaves

¼ teaspoon dried oregano

Salt and pepper, to taste

FOR BAGELWICHES:

4 bagels, split lengthwise

4 slices provolone cheese

24 fresh basil leaves

To make the filling: In a medium-size bowl, mash the chickpeas and avocado with a potato masher, or use a food processor. Add the yogurt, basil paste, oregano, salt, and pepper and stir to combine.

To make the bagelwiches: For each bagelwich, place a heaping scoop of the pesto filling on the bottom half of a bagel, add a slice of provolone and 6 fresh basil leaves, and top with the remaining bagel half. Slice in half and serve.

YIELD: 4 BAGELWICHES

← Artichoke, Kale & Mozzarella Melt

✳ Coconut Oil ✳ Kale

This Italian melt is a cross between a quesadilla and a pizza. When it's dipped in your favorite marinara sauce, you won't care what you call it, you'll just be in food bliss.

1 tablespoon (14 g) coconut oil

2 cups (140 g) diced, de-stemmed kale

2 teaspoons minced garlic

2 teaspoons balsamic vinegar

4 large tortillas, each buttered on one side

1 cup (120 g) grated mozzarella cheese

16 grape tomatoes

4 artichoke hearts, diced

1 cup (245 g) marinara sauce

In a medium-size skillet over medium heat, melt the coconut oil. Add the kale and garlic and sauté for approximately 5 minutes, until softened, and then add the balsamic vinegar and stir to combine.

On 2 tortillas, place a large handful of cheese and a generous scoop of the kale mixture, then 8 sliced grape tomatoes, 2 diced artichoke hearts, and another tortilla on top. Carefully transfer to a skillet set over medium heat (or assemble directly in the pan) and cook on both buttered sides until the tortilla is golden brown and the cheese is melted, 3 to 4 minutes per side. Slice into triangles.

Serve hot with a side of the marinara sauce for dipping.

YIELD: 2 MELTS

Sweet Potato Black Bean Quesadillas

✳ Sweet Potatoes ✳ Quinoa

This is another one of those combinations where I instantly thought, "Where have you been all my life?!" The sweet potato and black beans were meant to be together. Dip in salsa or the lime Greek yogurt sauce on page 111.

4 large tortillas, each buttered on one side

1 cup (120 g) shredded Cheddar cheese

1 large sweet potato, baked and flesh scooped out

1 (15-ounce, or 420 g) can black beans, rinsed and drained

2 tablespoons (24 g) cooked quinoa

On each of 2 tortillas, spread a large handful of cheese and a generous scoop of sweet potato, a layer of black beans (you may have some left over), 1 tablespoon (12 g) of the quinoa, and then another tortilla on top. Carefully transfer to a skillet set over medium heat (or assemble directly in the pan) and cook (on both buttered sides) until the tortilla is golden brown and cheese is melted, about 4 minutes on each side. Slice into triangles.

YIELD: 2 QUESADILLAS

BBQ Apple Cheddar Quesadillas

* Walnuts * Greek Yogurt

I'm convinced that the act of dipping in sauce significantly raises the likelihood of everyone in the family loving the meal. This dish is no exception. The barbecue–Greek yogurt dipping sauce is to-die-for, and the perfect tang for the apple Cheddar quesadillas.

FOR SAUCE:

¼ cup (60 g) Greek yogurt

¼ cup (60 g) barbecue sauce

FOR QUESADILLAS:

4 tortillas, each buttered on one side

1 cup (120 g) shredded Cheddar cheese

1 apple, peeled, cored, and sliced

4 slices cooked turkey bacon, torn into chunks

½ cup (60 g) coarsely chopped walnuts

To make the sauce: Combine both of the sauce ingredients in a small bowl.

To make the quesadillas: On each of 2 tortillas, place a large handful of cheese, a few apple slices, 2 slices of the bacon, and ¼ cup (30 g) of the walnuts, and then top with another tortilla.

Carefully transfer to a skillet set over medium heat (or assemble directly in the pan) and cook (on both buttered sides) until the tortilla is golden brown and the cheese is melted. Slice into triangles. Serve hot with the dipping sauce.

YIELD: 2 QUESADILLAS

Quinoa, Corn & Black Bean Quesadillas

❋ Coconut Oil ❋ Quinoa ❋ Greek Yogurt

There is something so comforting about the melted cheesy goodness of a quesadilla. The quinoa and black beans add both protein and substance to this simple meal. And once you taste the amazing yogurt sauce, you will want to dip everything in it and then lick the bowl clean!

FOR QUESADILLAS:

1 tablespoon (14 g) coconut oil

¼ onion, diced

1 cup (185 g) cooked quinoa

1 cup (130 g) sweet corn kernels

1 cup (240 g) black beans, rinsed and drained

1 tablespoon (15 g) green chile salsa or your favorite salsa

Juice of ½ lime

½ teaspoon ground cumin

8 small flour tortillas, each buttered on one side

2 cups (240 g) shredded Cheddar or Jack cheese

FOR SAUCE:

¾ cup (172 g) plain Greek yogurt

Juice of ½ lime

To make the quesadillas: In a large skillet, melt the coconut oil. Add the onion and sauté for approximately 5 minutes, until the onion is softened and lightly browned. Add the quinoa, corn, black beans, salsa, lime juice, and cumin. Stir to combine. Sauté over medium heat for approximately 5 minutes, or until lightly browned and heated through. Remove from the heat.

For each quesadilla, place a large handful of cheese and a generous scoop of the quinoa-corn mixture on a tortilla, then top with another tortilla. Carefully transfer to a skillet set over medium heat (or assemble directly in the pan) and cook (on both buttered sides) until the tortilla is golden brown and the cheese is melted, 3 or 4 minutes per side. Repeat with the remaining tortillas. Slice into triangles.

To make the sauce: In a small bowl, combine the sauce ingredients. Serve alongside the quesadillas for dipping.

YIELD: 4 QUESADILLAS

Quinoa Fiesta Wrap

✳ Greek Yogurt ✳ Honey ✳ Quinoa

All of my favorite things are stuffed into one wrap and then drizzled with an amazing sauce. I could eat this every single day! Make it breakfast-worthy by adding in scrambled eggs.

FOR SAUCE:

¼ cup (60 g) plain Greek yogurt

Juice of ½ lime

2 tablespoons (2 g) minced cilantro

1 teaspoon honey

¼ teaspoon ground cumin

2 tablespoons (18 g) crumbled goat cheese (optional)

FOR WRAPS:

4 large tortillas

1 (15-ounce, or 420 g) can black beans, rinsed and drained

1 cup (185 g) cooked quinoa

2 avocados, peeled, pitted, and chopped

16 grape tomatoes, halved

To make the sauce: Combine the sauce ingredients in a small bowl, smashing the goat cheese with a fork and blending well.

To make the wraps: In the center of each tortilla place one-fourth each of the black beans, quinoa, avocados, tomatoes, and sauce. Fold the sides of the tortilla in, fold the bottom over the filling, and roll.

YIELD: 4 WRAPS

main *dishes*

From mac and cheese, to burgers, to Chinese food, to pizza, these favorite dinners are now packed with super-foods. But everyone will gobble them up just the same!

Honey Sesame Fish Tacos with Lime Greek Yogurt Sauce

* Greek Yogurt * Honey

I absolutely LOVE fish tacos. Like I am totally obsessed, cannot pass them up on a menu at a restaurant, could eat them every single day for the rest of my life . . . yum! And I feel great about serving them to my family because they include protein, veggies, and Greek yogurt—all in one meal!

FOR SAUCE:

¾ cup (172 g) plain Greek yogurt

Juice of ½ lime

FOR TACOS:

2 tablespoons (30 ml) sesame oil

2 tablespoons (40 g) honey

2 tablespoons (30 ml) soy sauce

1 teaspoon molasses

¼ teaspoon chili powder

¼ teaspoon garlic powder

¼ teaspoon red cayenne pepper

12 ounces (336 g) cod, thawed if frozen

8 white corn tortillas

1 cup (120 g) shredded Cheddar or Jack cheese

¼ purple cabbage, shredded

To make the sauce: In a small bowl, combine the yogurt and lime juice. Set aside.

To make the tacos: Combine the sesame oil, honey, soy sauce, molasses, chili powder, garlic powder, and cayenne pepper in a medium-size sauté pan over medium heat. Stir to blend. Add the fish and cook for approximately 15 minutes, until the fish is opaque in the center and flakes easily with a fork. Chop the cooked fish in the pan so that it's diced and more thoroughly covered with sauce.

Serve the cooked fish with the tortillas, cheese, purple cabbage, and yogurt sauce.

YIELD: 8 TACOS

USING UP INGREDIENTS

When I buy more unusual ingredients, such as purple cabbage, I like to have a couple of recipes on hand to make that week so that none of it goes to waste. Use any leftover cabbage from this fish taco recipe to make the Chopped Purple Power Salad on page 83.

Shrimp Fried "Rice"

✱ Coconut Oil ✱ Eggs ✱ Quinoa ✱ Honey

Usually when I go out to an Asian restaurant, I pick the healthier meal accompaniment: brown rice over the usual white. But this meal takes it one step further, using quinoa as the base. Beautiful and bursting with flavor and nutrients, it's like takeout, but better. And it's faster, too!

1 tablespoon (14 g) coconut oil, divided

3 eggs

4 cups (740 g) cooked quinoa

¾ cup (112 g) peas

1 carrot, julienned

⅓ cup (50 g) diced water chestnuts

12 ounces (336 g) deveined, tail-off medium-size shrimp, cooked

1 teaspoon minced garlic

2 tablespoons (30 ml) rice vinegar

2 tablespoons (30 ml) soy sauce

2 tablespoons (30 ml) teriyaki sauce

1 teaspoon honey

In a large skillet over medium heat, melt 1½ teaspoons (7 g) of the coconut oil. Crack in the eggs and cook, stirring, until uniformly opaque, for 2 minutes. Use a spatula to flip the eggs over. Cook for an additional 1 to 2 minutes, then remove from the heat. Slice the cooked eggs into thin strips. Transfer to a bowl and reserve.

Melt the remaining 1½ teaspoons (7 g) coconut oil in the skillet. Add the quinoa, peas, carrot, water chestnuts, and shrimp to the skillet. In a small bowl, whisk together the garlic, vinegar, soy and teriyaki sauces, and honey. Pour into the skillet and stir to combine. Simmer over medium heat, stirring occasionally, for approximately 10 minutes, until the shrimp are warmed through.

YIELD: 4 SERVINGS

VEGETARIAN VERSION

This fried "rice" is great even without the shrimp. If you're vegetarian, leave out the shrimp and use some baby corn or cubed tofu instead.

Fiesta Stuffed Peppers

❋ Greek Yogurt ❋ Quinoa

I absolutely love bell peppers—raw, roasted, mixed into hummus, and more—but for some reason, I had never made a stuffed pepper before. These are now a weekly staple in my house (and belly).

8 ounces (227 g) grass-fed lean ground beef

¼ cup (40 g) diced yellow onion

½ cup (75 g) sweet corn kernels

Juice of ½ lime

1½ tablespoons (12 g) taco seasoning

1 cup (185 g) cooked quinoa

½ cup (120 g) refried black beans

2 tablespoons (30 g) Greek yogurt

4 bell peppers, tops sliced off and core, ribs, and seeds removed

Preheat the oven to 400°F (200°C, or gas mark 6). Line a baking sheet with aluminum foil.

In a large skillet over medium-high heat, add the ground beef, onion, corn, lime juice, and taco seasoning, stir to combine, and sauté until the onion is softened and the beef is no longer pink, about 8 minutes. Add the quinoa, refried beans, and Greek yogurt. Mix thoroughly.

Slice a tiny amount off the bottom of each pepper so it stands up easily, without cutting through to the inside. Stuff each pepper with the cooked beef mixture and stand them up on the prepared baking sheet. Bake for 25 minutes, until the bell peppers are softened and lightly browned. Serve hot.

YIELD: 4 STUFFED PEPPERS

The Best Sloppy Joes

❋ Honey ❋ Quinoa

Promise me you'll never buy canned Sloppy Joe mix again! It is loaded with high-fructose corn syrup. This homemade version is so easy, so fast, and so much better for you.

1 pound (454 g) grass-fed lean ground beef

½ teaspoon sea salt

1 cup (245 g) organic tomato sauce

½ cup (125 g) barbecue sauce

1 tablespoon (20 g) honey

1 teaspoon molasses

½ cup (92 g) cooked quinoa

4 hamburger buns

In a large skillet over medium-high heat, sauté the ground beef with the sea salt for approximately 8 minutes, until it is cooked through and no longer pink.

Add the tomato sauce, barbecue sauce, honey, molasses, and quinoa, stir to combine, and lower the heat to medium-low. Let it simmer for 20 minutes, stirring frequently, until slightly thickened.

Serve warm on the hamburger buns.

YIELD: 4 SANDWICHES

Hummus Meatloaf

It's hard to beat a good meatloaf, and this one is divine. Moist, flavorful, and delicious, this is a healthy spin on comfort food. Pair it with potato wedges to take it to the next level!

FOR MEATLOAF:

1 pound (454 g) grass-fed lean ground beef

2 eggs

1 cup (110 g) bread crumbs

1½ teaspoons Montreal steak seasoning

1 tablespoon (15 ml) Worcestershire sauce

2 tablespoons (30 g) ketchup

¼ cup (56 g) garlic hummus

1½ teaspoons molasses

FOR TOPPING:

⅓ cup (80 g) ketchup

⅓ cup (75 g) packed brown sugar

½ teaspoon dry mustard

To make the meatloaf: Preheat the oven to 400°F (200°C, or gas mark 6). Line a baking sheet with aluminum foil.

Combine all the meatloaf ingredients in a large mixing bowl. Use your hands to thoroughly combine the mixture, then form into a large ball. Place the ball on the prepared baking sheet and shape into a loaf.

To make the topping: Combine the topping ingredients in a small mixing bowl. Spoon the mixture over the meatloaf, covering it evenly.

Bake for 45 minutes, or until the meat is cooked through and no longer pink in the center. Remove from the oven and let rest for a few minutes before slicing.

YIELD: 4 TO 6 SERVINGS

Quinoa Meatballs Over Penne

> ✳ *Quinoa* ✳ *Eggs* ✳ *Coconut Oil*

The quinoa and crushed bagel crisps are the perfect addition to make these flavorful meatballs completely gluten-free. Flavored with garlic, basil, and red wine, these are anything but boring.

FOR MEATBALLS:

1 pound (454 g) grass-fed lean ground beef

2 teaspoons minced garlic

2 tablespoons (30 g) basil paste or 10 fresh basil leaves

1 teaspoon sea salt

½ cup (60 g) crushed gluten-free bagel crisps or bread crumbs

½ cup (92 g) cooked quinoa

1 egg

2 tablespoons (30 ml) red wine (I used Petite Sirah)

2 tablespoons (28 g) coconut oil

3 cups (780 g) spaghetti sauce

16 ounces (454 g) cooked penne

To make the meatballs: Combine the beef, garlic, basil paste, salt, bagel crisps, quinoa, egg, and red wine in a large mixing bowl. Use your hands to thoroughly combine, then form into 24 small meatballs.

In a large skillet over medium-high heat, melt the coconut oil. Add 8 to 10 meatballs at a time, placing them in a circle along the outer 2 inches (5 cm) of the pan. Let each side of the meatball cook for approximately 2 minutes, then turn them over, getting all sides evenly browned. Total cook time is about 8 minutes for each set of meatballs. Repeat with the remaining meatballs.

Once evenly browned, remove the meatballs from the skillet and add them to a stockpot along with the spaghetti sauce. Simmer the sauce and meatballs over medium-low heat for about 20 minutes. Serve over the cooked penne.

YIELD: 4 SERVINGS

BOOST THE NUTRITION WITH KALE

And if you happen to have any sauteed kale or other greens around, add it to the simmering spaghetti sauce. You will increase the nutrients without affecting the flavor too significantly!

Black Bean Quinoa Burgers

With flavors such as Worcestershire, Montreal steak seasoning, and ketchup, these quinoa burgers taste like the real deal. These are the veggie burgers that even meat lovers enjoy (and devour)!

1 (15-ounce, or 420 g) can black beans, rinsed and drained

1½ cups (278 g) cooked quinoa

1 egg

¼ cup (32 g) finely shredded carrot

¼ cup (38 g) finely shredded orange bell pepper

2 tablespoons (30 ml) Worcestershire sauce

1 teaspoon Montreal steak seasoning

1 teaspoon ground cumin

2 tablespoons (30 g) ketchup

½ cup (60 g) unbleached all-purpose flour

6 hamburger buns

6 slices cheese, for serving (optional)

12 slices turkey bacon, cooked, for serving (optional)

Sliced avocado, for serving (optional)

Sliced tomato, for serving (optional)

In a medium mixing bowl, mash the black beans with a fork. Add the quinoa, egg, carrot, bell pepper, Worcestershire, steak seasoning, cumin, ketchup, and flour and mix thoroughly with your hands. Chill in the refrigerator for at least 30 minutes to firm up a bit.

Preheat the oven to 350°F (180°C, or gas mark 4). Line a baking sheet with aluminum foil.

Remove the burger mixture from the refrigerator and form into 6 patties. Place on the prepared baking sheet and bake for 30 minutes, flipping the burgers halfway through, until the edges are lightly brown and the burgers cooked to your liking.

Serve each burger on a bun with 1 slice of cheese, 2 slices of turkey bacon, and some avocado and tomato slices, if desired.

YIELD: 6 BURGERS

SLIDERS FOR KIDS

Try baking the patties in a muffin tin to create mini sliders for a party, or for kids, or just for fun.

Orange Sesame Chicken

This homemade baked version of your favorite Chinese takeout (normally deep-fried) is healthier, yes, but it also rivals in flavor. The crunchy chicken tenders are coated in a thick orange sauce you will love!

FOR MARINADE:

1 cup (230 g) plain Greek yogurt
½ cup (120 ml) orange juice
2 tablespoons (30 ml) soy sauce
2 tablespoons (40 g) honey
½ teaspoon sea salt

1 pound (454 g) boneless, skinless organic chicken breasts, sliced into strips

FOR BREADING:

1 cup (120 g) flour
1 cup (115 g) bread crumbs
2 tablespoons (16 g) toasted sesame seeds

FOR SAUCE:

2 tablespoons (30 ml) sesame oil
2 tablespoons (30 ml) peanut oil
1 cup (235 ml) orange juice
2 tablespoons (16 g) cornstarch
1 cup (235 ml) chicken broth
1 teaspoon minced garlic
2 tablespoons (30 ml) soy sauce
1½ teaspoons sriracha
¼ cup (80 g) honey

Cooked white rice, for serving
Steamed broccoli, for serving

To make the marinade: Combine all of the marinade ingredients in a large zip-top bag. Seal and shake to blend. Add the chicken, seal the bag well, and massage the chicken to coat with the marinade. Place the bag in the refrigerator for at least 4 hours and up to 12 hours before cooking.

Preheat the oven to 375°F (190°C, or gas mark 5). Line a baking sheet with aluminum foil.

To make the breading: Combine the breading ingredients in a shallow dish. Whisk to blend.

Remove the chicken strips from the marinade, discarding the leftover marinade, and roll them one by one in the breading mixture. Place the chicken strips in a single layer on the prepared sheet. Bake for 25 minutes, flipping halfway through, until the chicken is opaque in the center with no pink remaining.

To make the sauce: Add the oils to a medium-size skillet over medium heat. Mix the orange juice and cornstarch together in a small cup, whisking until combined, then add it to the skillet. Stir in the broth, garlic, soy sauce, sriracha, and honey. Let the sauce simmer for approximately 15 minutes, stirring frequently, until thickened.

Add the cooked chicken strips to the heated sauce, turn to coat, remove with a slotted spoon, return them to the baking sheet, and bake for an additional 5 minutes, until the edges are crispy and lightly browned. Strain the remaining sauce into a gravy boat to remove any breading crumbs.

Serve warm with the rice, steamed broccoli, and orange sauce.

YIELD: 4 SERVINGS

Balsamic Kale & Chicken Sausage Pizza

* Chickpeas * Coconut Oil * Kale

With pizza being one of my husband's favorite foods, we have it almost weekly. He said he was completely surprised (and elated) by how much he loved this one, despite it having kale on it. As for the crust, it was absolutely perfect—a great backdrop for any pizza.

FOR CRUST:

1 cup (235 ml) hot water, approximately 120°F (49°C)

1½ teaspoons active dry yeast

1½ teaspoons sugar

½ cup (120 g) chickpeas, rinsed and drained

1½ teaspoons coconut oil, melted

½ teaspoon sea salt

1½ teaspoons dry ranch dressing mix

½ teaspoon dried oregano

½ teaspoon dried basil

2¼ cups (270 g) unbleached all-purpose flour

FOR PIZZA:

1 teaspoon coconut oil

1 cup (70 g) diced, de-stemmed kale

1 teaspoon balsamic vinegar

1 teaspoon basil paste or 6 fresh basil leaves

2 chicken sausages, sliced (I used basil-flavored ones)

¾ cup (185 g) pizza sauce

2 cups (240 g) shredded mozzarella cheese

To make the crust: Combine the hot water, active dry yeast, and sugar in a medium-size mixing bowl. Let the mixture sit for 15 minutes. The yeast should activate and become foamy.

Add the chickpeas and coconut oil to the yeast mixture. Use an immersion blender—a food processor or blender will also work—to puree until smooth. Add the salt, ranch mix, oregano, basil, and flour and mix thoroughly. Use your hands to roll it into a ball, kneading 2 or 3 times. Cover with plastic wrap and refrigerate for 4 to 8 hours before baking.

Preheat the oven to 425°F (220°C, or gas mark 7). Spray a baking sheet with nonstick spray or place a pizza stone in the oven to preheat.

To make the pizza: Turn the dough out onto a floured surface, and knead it 10 times. Use a rolling pin to flatten out the dough to 12 to 14 inches (30.5 to 35.5 cm) in diameter and ½ inch (1.3 cm) thick. Transfer to the prepared baking sheet or use a peel to transfer it to the hot pizza stone. Bake the crust for 10 minutes.

Meanwhile, in a medium-size skillet over medium heat, melt the coconut oil. Add the kale, balsamic vinegar, basil paste, and sliced chicken sausage. Sauté for approximately 5 minutes, or until the kale is softened and the sausage is heated through and lightly browned.

Remove the partially baked dough from the oven, spread the pizza sauce to within 1 inch (2.5 cm) of the edge, sprinkle on the cheese, and top with the sautéed kale and chicken sausage. Bake for an additional 10 minutes, or until the cheese is melted and lightly browned. Slice and serve hot.

YIELD: ONE 12- TO 14-INCH (30.5- TO 35.5-CM) PIZZA

Smoked Ham Pad Thai

* Coconut Oil * Sweet Potatoes * Honey * Chickpeas * Eggs

I have always loved pad Thai, with its flavor combination of sweet, salty, and nutty. This one is made healthier with the addition of chickpeas and sweet potato without sacrificing any delicious flavor!

FOR NOODLE BOWL:

1 teaspoon coconut oil

3 tablespoons (20 g) minced sweet potato

2 tablespoons (30 ml) sesame oil

2 tablespoons (30 ml) soy sauce

3 tablespoons (60 g) honey

1 tablespoon (15 ml) rice vinegar

1 tablespoon (8 g) minced garlic

Juice of ½ lime

1½ cups (225 g) diced smoked ham

1 carrot, sliced into thin rounds

¼ cup (38 g) diced orange bell pepper

2 eggs

1 (8-ounce, or 224 g) package rice noodles

FOR PEANUT SAUCE:

½ cup (130 g) peanut butter

½ cup (120 g) chickpeas, rinsed and drained

Juice of ½ lime

1 tablespoon (15 ml) soy sauce

3 tablespoons (60 g) honey

Carrot peels, for topping (optional)

To make the noodle bowl: Melt the coconut oil in a skillet over medium-high heat. Add the sweet potatoes and sauté for approximately 5 minutes, until softened. Add the sesame oil, soy sauce, honey, vinegar, garlic, and lime juice and stir to combine. Add the ham, carrot, and bell pepper and sauté for another 10 minutes, until lightly browned. Meanwhile, in another pan over medium heat, lightly scramble the eggs. Remove the pan from the heat, cut the eggs into strips, and add to the ham mixture.

Meanwhile, in a separate pot, bring a pot of water to a boil over medium-high heat. Add the noodles and remove from the heat. Let soak for 8 minutes, then drain. Transfer to a serving bowl and keep warm.

To make the sauce: Combine the ingredients in a large measuring cup. Use an immersion blender—a blender or food processor will also work—to puree until smooth.

Add the sauce to the noodles and toss to coat. Add the sautéed ham, vegetable and egg mixture, and toss to combine. Garnish with carrot peels, if desired.

YIELD: 4 TO 6 SERVINGS

Pork Tenderloin with Blueberry & Apple Compote

This is definitely the most delicious pork tenderloin I've ever eaten! The blueberries, apples, and honey give it a nice sweetness, while the cayenne and cinnamon give it a spicy kick. I love using some of the leftover compote as a gravy for the mashed potatoes.

FOR TENDERLOIN:

1 tablespoon (14 g) coconut oil, melted

1½ teaspoons lemon juice

1 tablespoon (15 ml) apple cider vinegar

1 tablespoon (8 g) minced garlic

2 tablespoons (30 ml) soy sauce

¼ cup (80 g) honey

¼ teaspoon ground cinnamon

⅛ teaspoon cayenne pepper

1⅓ pounds (605 g) pork tenderloin

1 cup (150 g) organic blueberries

½ cup (75 g) peeled and diced apple

FOR POTATOES:

3 large russet potatoes, peeled and cubed

¼ cup (½ stick, or 56 g) unsalted butter

2 tablespoons (30 g) plain Greek yogurt

2 tablespoons (30 ml) milk

½ teaspoon sea salt

½ teaspoon black pepper

To make the tenderloin: Combine the oil, lemon juice, vinegar, garlic, soy sauce, honey, cinnamon, and cayenne in a small bowl. Whisk to blend. Cut the tenderloin in half to make 2 smaller pieces. Place in a 9 x 9-inch (23 x 23-cm) baking dish, add the blueberries and apple, pour the sauce over all, turn to coat, and cover with foil. Marinate in the refrigerator for 4 hours and up to 8 hours.

Preheat the oven to 400°F (200°C, or gas mark 6). Remove the foil from the dish, transfer to the oven, and bake for 25 minutes. Remove briefly from the oven and spoon the sauce from the bottom of the pan on top of the tenderloin. Return the pan to the oven and bake for 25 minutes longer, or until the pork is opaque in the center and no pink remains.

To make the potatoes: Bring a pot of water to a boil over medium-high heat. Add the potatoes and boil for approximately 20 minutes, or until the potatoes are softened and are easily mashed with a fork.

Drain the potatoes and put them in a large mixing bowl. Add the butter and let melt, then add the yogurt, milk, salt, and pepper. Using a hand mixer, mix on medium-high speed until a smooth consistency is reached.

Serve the tenderloin hot with the mashed potatoes, spooning the sauce in the pan over the top.

YIELD: 4 SERVINGS

Spaghetti with Kale & Walnut Pesto

✱ Kale ✱ Walnuts

Creamy and bursting with flavor, this dish packs a full cup of kale per serving and is a great alternative to traditional pesto. It's also super easy to make: just blend everything in the food processor. It's colorful, healthy, and just plain fun, and Babycakes loves twirling these spaghetti noodles on her fork!

4 cups (280 g) diced, de-stemmed kale
1 cup (40 g) loosely packed fresh basil leaves
1½ cups (180 g) walnuts
½ cup (120 ml) olive oil
1 tablespoon (15 ml) white balsamic vinegar
½ red bell pepper, cored and chopped
½ cup (50 g) grated Parmesan cheese, plus more for serving
½ cup (60 g) grated Romano cheese
1 teaspoon dried oregano
1 tablespoon (8 g) minced garlic
16 ounces (454 g) spaghetti, uncooked
Salt and pepper, to taste
Fresh diced tomatoes, for serving (optional)

Combine the kale, basil, walnuts, oil, vinegar, bell pepper, cheeses, oregano, and garlic in a large food processor. Puree until smooth and creamy.

Bring a large pot of salted water to a boil over medium-high heat. Cook the pasta according to package directions, then drain, reserving about 1 cup (235 ml) of the pasta water, and place in a large serving bowl. Add half of the pesto, toss to combine, and taste. If you want it saucier, add more pesto. If it needs to be thinner, stir in some of the reserved pasta water. Season with salt and pepper.

Add the diced tomatoes and toss to combine. Pass the extra Parmesan cheese at the table.

YIELD: 4 TO 6 SERVINGS

Sweet Potato Mac & Cheese

✱ Sweet Potatoes ✱ Coconut Oil ✱ Greek Yogurt

A superfoods twist on a childhood favorite, this creamy macaroni and cheese will leave you asking for seconds. The sweet potato adds a mild flavor, but the cheese still dominates and shines through.

2 cups (200 g) pasta shells, uncooked

1½ cups (165 g) peeled and cubed sweet potato

⅓ cup (75 g) plain Greek yogurt

1 tablespoon (14 g) coconut oil, melted

1 tablespoon (15 ml) milk

½ cup (60 g) shredded American cheese

½ cup (60 g) shredded Swiss cheese

⅛ teaspoon sea salt

Pepper, to taste

Bring a medium-size stockpot of salted water to a boil over medium-high heat. Add the pasta shells and cook for 10 minutes, until the pasta is soft and cooked through.

Drain and remove the pasta from the stockpot, setting it aside for later. In the same stockpot, add the cubed sweet potato and 1 inch (2.5 cm) of water. Boil for approximately 6 minutes, or until the sweet potato is softened. Drain the water, then add the Greek yogurt, coconut oil, and milk. Use an immersion blender—a food processor will also work—to puree until smooth.

Return the stockpot to medium-low heat and stir in the cheeses and salt and pepper. Once melted, stir in the cooked pasta. Serve hot.

YIELD: 2 OR 3 SERVINGS

MAKE IT YOUR OWN

You can tailor this to your liking: add diced red bell pepper, steamed broccoli, or even a handful of smoked ham. You can also substitute cubed butternut squash for the sweet potato in the fall.

One-Pot Shrimp Orzo

❋ Coconut Oil ❋ Kale

I grew up with an Italian father who would get up at 4 a.m. on Sunday to make a batch of spaghetti and meatballs. Being the responsible and time-crunched daughter that I am, I took his secret recipe and tweaked it into this fabulous one-pot, 30-minute meal.

1 tablespoon (14 g) coconut oil

1 cup (70 g) diced, de-stemmed kale

1 tablespoon (8 g) minced garlic

2 cups (470 ml) chicken broth

1 (14-ounce, or 392 g) can fire-roasted tomatoes, with juice

⅓ cup (80 ml) olive oil

⅓ cup (80 ml) balsamic vinegar

1 teaspoon sea salt

1 teaspoon black pepper

¼ teaspoon dried basil

¼ teaspoon dried oregano

1 cup (160 g) uncooked organic orzo pasta

12 ounces (336 g) de-veined, tail-off medium-size shrimp

Parmesan cheese, for serving (optional)

In a large stockpot over medium heat, melt the coconut oil. Add the kale and garlic and sauté for approximately 5 minutes, until the kale is softened.

Add the broth, tomatoes and their juice, oil, vinegar, salt, pepper, basil, oregano, orzo, and shrimp; stir to combine and turn up the heat to high. Bring to a boil, then reduce the heat to medium and cook, uncovered, for 20 minutes, until the shrimp are opaque white and the orzo is soft.

Serve hot topped with the Parmesan cheese.

YIELD: 4 SERVINGS

One-Pot Teriyaki Noodles

✳ Honey ✳ Eggs

The beauty of this dish is the fact that you throw it all into one big pot and let it do its thing while you are free to accomplish whatever your heart desires. The Asian flavors are delicious, and with three full cups of fruits and veggies, you can feel great about serving it to your family!

⅓ cup (80 ml) each sesame oil and rice vinegar

2 cups (470 ml) chicken broth

1 tablespoon (20 g) honey

2 tablespoons (30 ml) each soy sauce and teriyaki sauce

½ teaspoon sriracha

1 teaspoon black pepper

¼ teaspoon sea salt

1 cup (155 g) diced pineapple

1 cup (125 g) diced water chestnuts

1 cup (75 g) sliced sugar snap peas

8 ounces (224 g) dried soba or ramen noodles

1 cup (175 g) diced raw chicken breast

4 eggs, beaten

In a large stockpot over medium-high heat, combine the oil, vinegar, broth, honey, soy sauce, teriyaki, sriracha, pepper, salt, pineapple, water chestnuts, sugar snap peas, and noodles. Stir to combine. Bring to a boil, then add the chicken breast and eggs, stirring to create ribbons with the egg.

Reduce the heat to medium low, and let simmer, uncovered, for 20 minutes, or until the chicken is opaque in the center and most of the liquid has been absorbed. Serve hot.

YIELD: 4 SERVINGS

desserts

We saved the best for last: pies, cobblers, and cookies . . . oh my! These desserts are decadent, fabulous, and quite possibly my favorite part of the book.

Chocolate Silk Pie

✳ Coconut Oil ✳ Eggs ✳ Greek Yogurt

I have made a lot of recipes over the years—thousands, probably—but my husband emphatically declared this to be his absolute favorite. The chocolate silky decadence, with a hint of coffee and coconut flavors, really makes this pie special. The hardest part is having patience while it sets in the fridge!

FOR CRUST:

2 cups (220 g) crushed graham crackers

6 tablespoons (84 g) coconut oil, melted

2 tablespoons (16 g) cocoa powder, plus extra as needed

1 egg

FOR FILLING:

1 cup (175 g) dark chocolate chips, melted

1 cup (230 g) plain Greek yogurt

3 egg yolks

¾ cup (150 g) coconut sugar

¼ cup (60 ml) brewed coffee

1 tablespoon (8 g) cornstarch

¼ cup (32 g) cocoa powder

1 teaspoon pure vanilla extract

¼ cup (56 g) coconut oil

1 cup (235 ml) heavy cream

½ cup (60 g) confectioners' sugar

Preheat the oven to 350°F (180°C, or gas mark 4).

To make the crust: Combine the crust ingredients in a large mixing bowl. Sprinkle a 9-inch (23-cm) pie pan with the extra cocoa powder, then press the crust mixture into the pan. Use extra cocoa powder if it is sticking to your hands. Be sure to press and fill the pan evenly. Bake for 12 minutes, until the crust is lightly browned, then remove from the oven and let cool.

To make the filling: In a medium-size saucepan over low heat, melt the dark chocolate chips. Add the yogurt, egg yolks, coconut sugar, coffee, cornstarch, cocoa, vanilla, and oil and stir to combine. Cook, stirring constantly, for approximately 10 minutes, or until the mixture is creamy, smooth, and thick.

Pour the filling into the pie crust. Let cool on the counter for about 30 minutes before putting it into the refrigerator. Refrigerate for 4 hours and up to 8 hours before adding the topping.

In a bowl with a whisk or handheld mixer, or in a stand mixer with the whisk attachment, beat the cream until soft peaks form. Add the confectioners' sugar and beat to combine. Spread in a thick layer over the top of the pie. Serve cold.

YIELD: ONE 9-INCH (23-CM) PIE

All-Natural Pecan Pie

✳ Eggs ✳ Honey ✳ Sweet Potatoes

This is a beautiful, rich, mouthwateringly delicious pecan pie that you can actually feel good about eating! The flavor is extraordinary, the texture perfect, and the likeness uncanny—all without corn syrup. I consider this a major success!

3 eggs

2 tablespoons (28 g) unsalted butter

¼ cup (60 ml) apple cider

¾ cup (150 g) coconut sugar

1 teaspoon pure vanilla extract

1 teaspoon ground ginger

1 tablespoon (15 ml) bourbon

1 teaspoon molasses

½ cup (160 g) honey

½ teaspoon salt

¼ cup (32 g) cornstarch

1 cup (110 g) peeled and cubed sweet potato

⅓ cup water

½ cup (120 ml) vanilla almond milk

2 cups (220 g) whole pecans

1 pie crust, homemade or store-bought

Preheat the oven to 375°F (190°C, or gas mark 5). Grease a 9-inch (23-cm) pie pan.

In a medium saucepan over low heat, combine the eggs, butter, cider, sugar, vanilla, ginger, bourbon, molasses, honey, salt, and cornstarch. Cook, stirring frequently, for 10 minutes, until thickened.

Place the sweet potatoes in a microwave-safe bowl, pour the water over, place a lid on top, and microwave on high for 4 minutes. Drain the water and add the almond milk. Use an immersion blender—a food processor or blender will also work—to puree until smooth. Add to the saucepan and stir to combine.

Stir in the pecans gently.

Line the prepared pie pan with the crust. Pour in the pie filling. Bake for 40 minutes, or until the pecans are lightly browned and the pie is set in the center.

Let cool before slicing.

YIELD: ONE 9-INCH (23-CM) PIE

Sweet Potato Pie with Maple Quinoa Crust

❋ Quinoa ❋ Sweet Potatoes ❋ Eggs

My family has always loved pumpkin pie during the holidays, but we will be making this sweet potato version instead for all future celebrations! It tastes divine, bakes up perfectly, and features a unique, superfood crust.

FOR CRUST:

1¾ cups (325 g) cooked quinoa

½ cup (60 g) unbleached all-purpose flour

2 tablespoons (14 g) ground flaxseed meal

¼ cup (60 ml) dark amber maple syrup

¼ cup (56 g) unsalted butter, at room temperature

FOR PIE FILLING:

4 cups (440 g) peeled and cubed sweet potato

1 cup (235 ml) almond milk

2 eggs

¾ cup (150 g) coconut sugar

1 teaspoon ground cinnamon

¼ teaspoon ground cloves

¼ teaspoon ground ginger

Preheat the oven to 400°F (200°C, or gas mark 6). Grease a 9-inch (23-cm) pie pan.

To make the crust: Combine the quinoa, flour, flaxseed meal, and maple syrup in a medium-size mixing bowl. Use a fork to fold in the butter. Mix thoroughly and evenly. Press the quinoa crust into the prepared pie pan. Bake the crust for 10 minutes, then remove from the heat.

To make the filling: Bring a pot of water to a boil over medium-high heat. Add the sweet potatoes and cook for approximately 20 minutes, until softened. Drain.

Add the sweet potatoes to a large mixing bowl with the almond milk. Use an immersion blender—a food processor or blender will also work—to puree until smooth. Add the eggs, sugar, cinnamon, cloves, and ginger and stir to combine.

Pour the mixture into the partially baked quinoa crust. Return the pie to the oven and bake for 1 hour, or until a knife inserted into the center comes out clean. Check on the crust partway through to make sure it's not getting too dark. If it is, add foil around the edges to protect it while the pie finishes baking.

YIELD: ONE 9-INCH (23-CM) PIE

Very Berry Cobbler with Quinoa

* Blueberries * Honey * Quinoa * Greek Yogurt * Coconut Oil * Eggs

Simmering the berries in a mixture of Kahlúa, coconut sugar, and vanilla brings such a unique taste to this dessert. Any possible tartness from the berries is wiped away and replaced with a smooth, rich sweetness. Filled with antioxidants and six of the superfoods, this is one dessert that you don't have to feel guilty about taking another bite.

FOR BERRY FILLING:

2 cups (300 g) organic blueberries, frozen or fresh

2 cups (300 g) organic blackberries

1 teaspoon pure vanilla extract

2 tablespoons (40 g) honey

2 tablespoons (30 ml) water

1 tablespoon (8 g) cornstarch

2 teaspoons Kahlúa (optional)

FOR COBBLER TOPPING:

1 cup (185 g) cooked quinoa

¼ cup (58 g) plain Greek yogurt

¼ cup (56 g) coconut oil, melted

2 tablespoons (40 g) honey

2 egg yolks

2 teaspoons baking powder

½ teaspoon sea salt

1 cup (120 g) unbleached all-purpose flour

⅓ cup (66 g) coconut sugar

Vanilla ice cream, for serving (optional)

Preheat the oven to 375°F (190°C, or gas mark 5). Grease a 6 x 9 x 3-inch (15 x 23 x 7.5-cm) baking dish.

To make the filling: Combine all the filling ingredients in a medium-size stockpot over medium-low heat. Simmer for approximately 10 minutes, until the berries are softened and the mixture is homogenous.

To make the topping: Combine the quinoa, yogurt, oil, honey, and egg yolks in a large mixing bowl. Stir to thoroughly combine. In a separate bowl, whisk together the baking powder, salt, flour, and sugar. Add to the wet ingredients and stir to combine.

Pour the berry filling into the prepared baking dish. Spoon on the cobbler topping, leaving some areas with berries showing through. Bake for 45 minutes, or until the topping is golden brown and the berry mixture is bubbly.

Scoop into bowls and serve hot, with vanilla ice cream.

YIELD: 6 SERVINGS

Dark Chocolate Cupcakes with Peanut Butter Cream Cheese Frosting

* Chickpeas * Greek Yogurt

Is there anything richer and more flavorful than the combination of chocolate and peanut butter? Infused with Greek yogurt in (and on) the cupcakes, this is one dark chocolate–peanut butter dessert you don't have to feel guilty about.

FOR CUPCAKES:

½ cup (120 g) chickpeas, rinsed and drained

1 cup (235 ml) vanilla almond milk

½ cup (115 g) plain Greek yogurt

1 teaspoon pure vanilla extract

1 cup (200 g) coconut sugar

6 tablespoons (48 g) cocoa powder

1½ cups (180 g) unbleached all-purpose flour

2 teaspoons baking powder

1 cup (175 g) dark chocolate chips

FOR FROSTING:

¾ cup (172 g) plain Greek yogurt

½ cup (130 g) peanut butter

½ cup (115 g) cream cheese

1 cup (120 g) confectioners' sugar

Preheat the oven to 350°F (180°C, or gas mark 4). Line a cupcake tin with paper cupcake liners.

To make the cupcakes: Combine the chickpeas and almond milk in a large measuring cup. Use an immersion blender—a food processor or blender will also work—to puree the mixture until smooth.

Combine the chickpea mixture, yogurt, vanilla, and coconut sugar in a large mixing bowl. Stir to blend. In a separate bowl, combine the cocoa powder, flour, and baking powder. Whisk to blend. Add to the wet ingredients and stir to combine. Fold in the chocolate chips.

Divide the batter evenly among the cupcake liners. Bake for 25 minutes, or until a toothpick inserted into the center comes out clean and the top of the cupcake springs back when lightly touched with the fingertips. Remove from the oven and place on a wire rack to cool completely.

To make the frosting: Combine the yogurt, peanut butter, cream cheese, and confectioners' sugar in a large mixing bowl. Use a hand mixer to blend until smooth and creamy. Transfer to a frosting bag and pipe onto the top of each cupcake. Serve immediately.

YIELD: 12 CUPCAKES

MAKE YOUR OWN FROSTING BAG

If you don't have a traditional frosting bag, use a plastic zip-top bag instead. Scoop the frosting into the bag, pushing it toward one of the bottom corners. Then, use a pair of scissors to cut a small triangle off the corner. Squeeze the frosting out of the corner to pipe.

Lemon Cupcakes with Blueberry Buttercream Frosting

✳ Eggs ✳ Greek Yogurt ✳ Honey ✳ Blueberries

I measure the success of a cupcake by how light and fluffy it is. These were just that, a true cupcake, even with the addition of protein-rich Greek yogurt! Topped with a blueberry buttercream frosting and adorned with a dried blueberry, they're almost too cute to eat . . . almost.

FOR CUPCAKES:

½ cup (1 stick, or 112 g) unsalted butter

1 cup (200 g) granulated sugar

3 eggs

¾ cup (172 g) plain Greek yogurt

2 tablespoons (30 ml) lemon juice

1 tablespoon (6 g) lemon zest

¼ cup (80 g) honey

2½ cups (300 g) unbleached all-purpose flour

1 tablespoon (8 g) baking powder

¼ teaspoon sea salt

1 cup (235 ml) vanilla almond milk

FOR FROSTING:

1 cup (2 sticks, or 225 g) butter, at room temperature

5 cups (600 g) confectioners' sugar

2 tablespoons (30 ml) blueberry juice (I used the juice from thawed frozen blueberries)

2 tablespoons (30 ml) vanilla almond milk

12 dried blueberries, for garnish

Preheat the oven to 350°F (180°C, or gas mark 4). Line a cupcake tin with paper cupcake liners.

To make the cupcakes: Partially melt the butter in the microwave for 30 seconds, then add to a bowl along with the sugar and eggs, and beat with a hand mixer until fluffy. Add the yogurt, lemon juice, lemon zest, and honey and stir to combine.

In a separate bowl, whisk together the flour, baking powder, and salt. Add to the wet ingredients, alternating with the milk, in 2 batches, beginning and ending with the milk, and blend until smooth.

Divide the cupcake batter among the paper liners. Bake for 20 minutes, until a toothpick inserted into the center comes out clean. Remove from the oven and place on a wire rack to cool.

To make the frosting: Combine the ingredients in a large mixing bowl, using a hand mixer to blend until creamy and fluffy. Transfer to a frosting bag and pipe onto the top of each cupcake. Top with a dried blueberry.

Serve immediately.

YIELD: 12 CUPCAKES

Mini Cheesecakes with Blueberries

✳ Walnuts ✳ Honey ✳ Coconut Oil ✳ Greek Yogurt ✳ Eggs ✳ Blueberries

These little cheesecakes are so tasty and versatile. You can make them individualized by adding different toppings: frozen blueberries, diced strawberries, mini chocolate chips, raspberries, a dollop of peanut butter—the possibilities are endless!

FOR CRUST:

¾ cup (112 g) chopped walnuts

½ cup (90 g) pitted, chopped dates (approximately 6)

½ cup (55 g) crushed graham crackers

3 tablespoons (42 g) unsalted butter

1 tablespoon (20 g) honey

FOR CHEESECAKE:

1 cup (175 g) white chocolate chips

3 tablespoons (42 g) coconut oil

1 cup (230 g) plain Greek yogurt

3 egg yolks

¾ cup (150 g) sugar

8 ounces (224 g) cream cheese

1 tablespoon (15 ml) pure vanilla extract

1 tablespoon (8 g) cornstarch

¾ cup (112 g) blueberries

Preheat the oven to 350°F (180°C, or gas mark 4). Spray the cups of a muffin tin with nonstick spray.

To make the crust: Combine all the crust ingredients in a food processor. Blend until combined. Press the crust into each of the muffin cups. Bake for 12 minutes, then remove from the heat.

To make the cheesecake: In a medium saucepan over low heat, melt the chocolate chips and coconut oil. Stir in the yogurt, egg yolks, sugar, cream cheese, vanilla, and cornstarch. Cook, stirring continually, for 10 minutes, until thickened.

Divide the cheesecake filling evenly among the muffin cups, filling almost to the top. Drop a few blueberries into the center of each cheesecake. Let cool for 20 minutes on the counter, then transfer to the freezer overnight.

Carefully run a knife along the edge of each cheesecake to remove from the muffin tin. Serve cold.

YIELD: 12 MINI CHEESECAKES

EASY RELEASE TIP

To make it easier to get the cheesecakes out of the tin after freezing, cut small, 5-inch (12.5-cm) strips of parchment paper to lay in the bottom of each muffin cup before adding the crust. After they're done in the freezer, just grab the ends of the parchment strip and lift up the cheesecake!

Banana Nut White Chocolate Cake

✳ Chickpeas ✳ Walnuts

This cake is nutritious enough to serve as a breakfast cake with coffee and sweet enough to serve as a decadent dessert with a scoop of ice cream. It is rich, moist, and delicious! Try topping it with the peanut butter cream cheese frosting on page 146 for a classic combo of peanut butter and banana.

1 cup (240 g) chickpeas, rinsed and drained

½ cup (120 ml) vanilla almond milk

½ cup (1 stick, or 112 g) unsalted butter

¾ cup (150 g) sugar

½ cup (112 g) mashed banana

1½ cups (180 g) unbleached all-purpose flour

½ teaspoon ground cinnamon

1 teaspoon baking soda

½ cup (60 g) coarsely chopped walnuts

1 cup (175 g) white chocolate chips

Preheat the oven to 375°F (190°C, or gas mark 5). Grease a 6 x 9 x 3-inch (15 x 23 x 7.5-cm) baking dish.

Combine the chickpeas and almond milk in a large measuring cup. Use an immersion blender—a food processor or blender will also work—to puree until smooth.

In a large mixing bowl, combine the chickpea puree, butter, sugar, and banana, stirring until smooth. In a separate bowl whisk together the flour, cinnamon, and baking soda. Add to the wet ingredients and stir to combine. Fold in the walnuts and chocolate chips.

Pour the batter into the prepared baking dish, and bake for 45 minutes, or until a knife inserted into the center comes out clean.

Serve warm.

YIELD: 9 SERVINGS

Chocolate-Covered Strawberry Bread

❋ Coconut Oil ❋ Kale! ❋ Eggs

This bread is not just stunningly beautiful on the outside, with sliced, roasted strawberries and drizzled chocolate all over, but it is also healthy on the inside, with greens hidden in the batter! And don't worry, the bitterness of the kale is eliminated when it is lightly sautéed in coconut oil before being added to the batter. The final result is a richer tasting—and healthier—bread.

FOR BREAD:

2 tablespoons (14 g) coconut oil

½ cup (35 g) diced, de-stemmed kale

½ cup (1 stick, or 112 g) unsalted butter

¾ cup (180 ml) vanilla almond milk

2 egg yolks

⅔ cup (132 g) coconut sugar

2 cups (240 g) unbleached all-purpose flour

¼ cup (32 g) cocoa powder

1 tablespoon (8 g) baking powder

½ teaspoon sea salt

¾ cup (128 g) hulled and diced strawberries plus 2 strawberries, hulled and sliced, divided

1 cup (175 g) dark chocolate chips

FOR TOPPING:

½ cup (90 g) dark chocolate chips

1 teaspoon vanilla almond milk

Preheat the oven to 375°F (190°C, or gas mark 5). Spray a 9 x 5 x 3-inch (23 x 12.5 x 7.5-cm) loaf pan with nonstick spray.

To make the bread: In a small skillet over medium-low heat, melt the coconut oil. Add the kale and sauté for approximately 3 minutes, until the kale is softened. Remove from the heat.

Partially melt the butter in the microwave for 30 seconds. In a large mixing bowl, combine the sautéed kale, butter, milk, egg yolks, and sugar. Stir thoroughly until well mixed.

In a separate bowl, whisk together the flour, cocoa powder, baking powder, and salt. Add to the wet ingredients and stir to combine. Fold in the diced strawberries and chocolate chips. Pour the batter into the prepared loaf pan.

Lay the remaining strawberry slices flat on top of the bread batter. Press lightly to make sure they stick.

Bake the bread for 70 minutes, or until a knife inserted into the center comes out clean. Let cool for 1 hour in the pan, then run a knife around the edges of the pan and turn out the loaf onto a wire rack. Lay a piece of parchment paper under the rack for easy cleanup.

To make the topping: In a small saucepan over low heat, melt the chocolate chips and almond milk. Stir to blend. Dip a fork into the sauce and drizzle the melted chocolate mixture on top of the cooled loaf.

YIELD: 1 LOAF

Superfood Chocolate Chip Cookies

* Chickpeas * Eggs

I'm not going to lie. This was the hardest recipe in the book. It took me four or five iterations to perfect it. Why? Because I wanted a true classic chocolate chip cookie: not too fluffy or cakey, not too chewy but also not too crisp. This is the only chocolate chip cookie recipe you'll need from now on!

½ cup (120 g) chickpeas, rinsed and drained

¼ cup (60 ml) vanilla almond milk

½ cup (1 stick, or 112 g) unsalted butter

½ cup (100 g) granulated sugar

½ cup (100 g) coconut sugar

1 teaspoon pure vanilla extract

2 egg yolks

1 teaspoon cornstarch

1 teaspoon baking soda

1½ cups (180 g) unbleached all-purpose flour

½ teaspoon sea salt

1¾ cups (306 g) dark chocolate chips

Preheat the oven to 350°F (180°C, or gas mark 4). Line 2 baking sheets with parchment paper.

Combine the chickpeas and almond milk in a large measuring cup. Use an immersion blender—a food processor or blender will also work—to puree until smooth.

Partially melt the butter in the microwave for 30 seconds. In a large bowl, use a hand mixer to thoroughly combine the chickpea mixture, butter, sugars, vanilla, and egg yolks.

In a separate bowl, whisk together the cornstarch, baking soda, flour, and salt. Add to the wet ingredients and stir to combine. Fold in the chocolate chips.

Use a spoon to form 1½-inch (3.8-cm) balls. You should get about 24 balls. Place 6 to 8 on each prepared baking sheet. Bake for 10 minutes, rotating the pans halfway through, until lightly golden brown and set in the center. Let cool on the baking sheets before transferring to a wire rack to cool completely. Repeat with the remaining dough balls.

YIELD: 24 COOKIES

Quinoa Brownies

* *Sweet Potatoes* * *Quinoa* * *Honey* * *Eggs*

Shhhhh! My husband raved about these brownies, but he had no idea there was quinoa *and* sweet potato hidden inside. It'll be our little secret. These brownies, though packed with superfoods, will be remembered and praised as being decadent and delicious, not "healthy."

½ cup (55 g) peeled and cubed sweet potato

⅓ cup (80 ml) water

⅓ cup (80 ml) vanilla almond milk

1 cup (185 g) cooked quinoa

1 teaspoon honey

1 egg

3 tablespoons (42 g) unsalted butter, melted

⅔ cup (132 g) coconut sugar

¼ cup (25 g) rolled oats

¾ cup (80 g) unbleached all-purpose flour

1 teaspoon baking powder

3 tablespoons (24 g) cocoa powder

1½ cups (262 g) dark chocolate chips

Preheat the oven to 375°F (190°C, or gas mark 5). Grease a 9 x 9-inch (23 x 23-cm) baking pan.

Place the sweet potatoes in a microwave-safe bowl, pour the water over, place a lid on top, and microwave on high power for 4 minutes. Drain the water and add the almond milk. Use an immersion blender—a food processor or blender will also work—to puree until smooth.

Combine the pureed sweet potato, quinoa, honey, egg, butter, and sugar in a large bowl. Stir until thoroughly combined.

In a separate bowl, whisk together the oats, flour, baking powder, and cocoa powder. Add to the wet ingredients and stir to combine. Fold in the chocolate chips.

Pour the batter into the baking dish, and bake for 30 minutes, or until a knife inserted into the center comes out clean. Let cool before slicing into nine 3 x 3-inch (7.5 x 7-cm) squares.

Serve warm.

YIELD: 9 BROWNIES

SUBSTITUTION SUGGESTION

If you're out of sweet potatoes, you can substitute cubed butternut squash.

Double Chocolate Swirl Brownies

* Chickpeas * Eggs * Greek Yogurt

These brownies are simple to make yet look fancy. Each bite is absolutely delicious with the swirls of chocolate and cream cheese. Take your brownies to a whole new level and never buy a boxed mix again!

FOR BROWNIE BATTER:

¾ cup (180 g) chickpeas, rinsed and drained

1½ cups (355 ml) vanilla almond milk

1¼ cups (250 g) coconut sugar

1½ teaspoons pure vanilla extract

3 eggs

½ cup (60 g) cocoa powder

3 cups (360 g) unbleached all-purpose flour

1½ teaspoons baking powder

1½ teaspoons baking soda

1½ cups (262 g) dark chocolate chips

FOR CREAM CHEESE FILLING:

8 ounces (224 g) cream cheese

1 teaspoon pure vanilla extract

½ cup (115 g) plain Greek yogurt

¼ cup (50 g) granulated sugar

1 egg

Preheat the oven to 350°F (180°C, or gas mark 4). Grease a 12 x 8-inch (30 x 20-cm) baking pan.

To make the brownie batter: Combine the chickpeas and almond milk in a large measuring cup. Use an immersion blender—a food processor or blender will also work—to puree until smooth. Add to a large bowl along with the coconut sugar, vanilla, and eggs. Stir to combine.

In a separate bowl, whisk together the cocoa, flour, baking powder, and baking soda. Add to the wet ingredients and stir to combine. Fold in the chocolate chips.

To make the cream cheese filling: Combine all the filling ingredients in a medium-size mixing bowl. Use a hand mixer to beat until smooth.

Spoon two-thirds of the brownie batter into the prepared pan. Then, spoon all of the cream cheese batter on top of that, spreading evenly with a spoon. Finally, spoon the final one-third of the brownie batter in clumps on top, leaving a lot of the cream cheese batter showing through.

Take a knife and run it through the batters to swirl the brownie batter and the cream cheese batter. Run the knife left to right, then up and down, then repeat one more time.

Bake for 55 minutes, or until a knife inserted into the center comes out clean. Let cool, then cut into 2 x 2-inch (5 x 5-cm) squares.

YIELD: 24 BROWNIES

Dessert Hummus

* Chickpeas * Honey

Don't let the name of this recipe throw you off. This is more dessert-y than hummus-y. The sweet creamy goodness will have you grabbing for that next animal cracker (or spoon). Instead of chocolate chips, try adding 2 teaspoons ground cinnamon and ½ cup (75 g) raisins. Or sweeten up the original version even more with the addition of mashed banana.

2 (15-ounce, or 420 g) cans
chickpeas, rinsed and drained
¼ cup (80 g) honey
¼ cup (60 ml) vanilla almond milk
¼ cup (65 g) peanut butter
¼ cup (25 g) confectioners' sugar
½ cup (90 g) chocolate chips
Animal crackers, for serving

Add the chickpeas, honey, milk, peanut butter, confectioners' sugar, and chocolate chips to a food processor. Blend until thoroughly combined and a smooth consistency.

Serve with the animal crackers for dipping.

YIELD: 2 CUPS (450 G)

Lemon Kiss Quinoa Cookies

* Quinoa * Eggs

Super light and refreshing, these lemon cookies are like kissing the sun. The zesty fresh lemon taste paired with the sweetness of the sugar and white chocolate make a powerful combination!

½ cup (1 stick, or 112 g) unsalted butter

¾ cup (140 g) cooked quinoa

½ cup (120 ml) almond milk

1 cup (200 g) sugar

3 tablespoons (45 ml) lemon juice

1 tablespoon (6 g) lemon zest

2 egg yolks

1 teaspoon cornstarch

2 teaspoons baking soda

1½ cups (180 g) unbleached all-purpose flour

1 cup (175 g) white chocolate chips

Preheat the oven to 350°F (180°C, or gas mark 4). Line 2 baking sheets with parchment paper.

Partially melt the butter in the microwave for 30 seconds. In a large mixing bowl, combine the butter, quinoa, milk, sugar, lemon juice and zest, and eggs. Stir thoroughly until well mixed.

In a separate bowl, whisk together the cornstarch, baking soda, and flour. Add to the wet ingredients and stir to combine. Fold in the chocolate chips.

Use a spoon to form 1½-inch (3.8-cm) balls. You should get about 24 balls. Place 6 to 8 on each prepared baking sheet. Bake for 15 minutes, rotating the pans halfway through, until lightly golden brown and set in the center. Let cool on the baking sheets before transferring to a wire rack to cool completely. Repeat with the remaining dough balls.

YIELD: 24 COOKIES

Mocha Pistachio Bark with Toasted Quinoa

❋ Quinoa ❋ Coconut Oil

This is like a healthy version of a Nestlé Crunch bar! It is delightfully light and melts in your mouth. My coworker said she was going to nibble on it throughout the day; five minutes later she confessed she'd devoured it all . . . it's that good!

⅓ cup (58 g) uncooked quinoa

3 cups (525 g) dark chocolate chips

1½ teaspoons coconut oil, melted

1 tablespoon (15 ml) brewed coffee

1 teaspoon pure vanilla extract

⅓ cup (50 g) dried cranberries

⅓ cup (50 g) coarsely chopped pistachios

Preheat the oven to 400°F (200°C, or gas mark 6). Line 2 baking sheets with parchment paper.

Spread the quinoa on one of the prepared baking sheets and toast for 10 minutes, then remove from the oven to cool.

Meanwhile, melt the chocolate chips in the top of a double boiler or in a stainless steel mixing bowl set over a pot of simmering water (make sure the bottom of the bowl doesn't touch the water). Once they are melted completely, stir in the coconut oil, coffee, and vanilla. Mix thoroughly.

Pour the mixture onto the second prepared baking sheet. Use a spoon to flatten and level the mixture. Sprinkle the dried cranberries and pistachios evenly over the top, pressing them down gently with your hand or the back of a spoon.

Cool for 1 hour in the refrigerator, then break apart into pieces and enjoy! Store in an airtight container in the refrigerator.

YIELD: APPROXIMATELY 36 SMALL PIECES

LITTLE HELPERS

These bark recipes are great for getting your kids involved in the kitchen. My daughter loved sprinkling on the toppings and then gently pressing them into the bark. She really focused on spreading out the ingredients evenly and loved being a part of the process!

Orange Butterscotch Bark with Dried Blueberries and Walnuts

> * Walnuts * Coconut Oil * Blueberries

Besides being absolutely gorgeous and a perfect homemade gift for family or friends, this bark is melt-in-your-mouth delicious! The orange gives it a burst of citrusy freshness, the walnuts give it a nice crunch, and the blueberries a little added sweetness. Though you'll probably want to eat the entire plate, remember that small portions of treats are best for both your body and your psyche!

⅓ cup (50 g) walnuts

3 cups (525 g) butterscotch chips

1 tablespoon (14 g) coconut oil, melted

2 tablespoons (30 ml) orange juice or juice of 1 clementine

1 teaspoon orange zest

1 teaspoon pure vanilla extract

1 cup (150 g) dried organic blueberries

Preheat the oven to 400°F (200°C, or gas mark 6). Line 2 baking sheets with parchment paper.

Spread the walnuts on one of the prepared baking sheets and toast for 10 minutes, then remove from the oven to cool.

Meanwhile, melt the butterscotch chips in the top of a double boiler or in a stainless steel mixing bowl set over a pot of simmering water (make sure the bottom of the bowl doesn't touch the water). Once melted completely, stir in the coconut oil, orange juice, orange zest, vanilla, and walnuts. Mix thoroughly.

Pour the mixture onto the second prepared baking sheet. Use a spoon to flatten and level the mixture. Sprinkle the dried blueberries evenly over the top, pressing them down gently with your hand or the back of a spoon.

Cool for 1 hour in the refrigerator, then break apart into pieces and enjoy! Store in an airtight container in the refrigerator.

YIELD: APPROXIMATELY 36 SMALL PIECES

Blueberry Creamsicles

* Chickpeas * Greek Yogurt * Honey * Blueberries

I don't know why, but I was always intimidated by the thought of making ice pops at home. But they're so easy! It literally takes five minutes to stir together, then just pop them in the freezer. A few hours later you have a creamy treat that your entire family will love. So, here's to more summer days eating creamsicles on the patio!

½ cup (120 g) chickpeas, rinsed and drained

½ cup (120 ml) vanilla almond milk

1 cup (230 g) plain Greek yogurt

1 teaspoon pure vanilla extract

1 teaspoon honey

½ cup (75 g) organic blueberries, frozen or fresh

Combine the chickpeas and vanilla almond milk in a large measuring cup. Use an immersion blender—a food processor or blender will also work—to puree until smooth.

Combine the chickpea mixture, yogurt, vanilla, and honey in a small mixing bowl. Stir to combine. Fold in the blueberries.

Pour into 6 ice pop molds. Put in the freezer for at least 4 hours before serving.

YIELD: 6 CREAMSICLES

MIX-IN SUGGESTIONS

You can make all sorts of flavor variations by mixing in different fruits. Try diced strawberries with 1 tablespoon (15 ml) lemon juice, or diced peaches with cocoa powder and pistachios.

acknowledgments

To Mary, director of digital sales at Fair Winds Press, thank you for seeing something in me and forwarding on my initial email to your acquiring cookbook editor at 7 p.m. on a Friday. Without you, this book never would have happened!

To Amanda and Winnie, my editor and publisher, thank you for believing in this book from the beginning, but more than that, for believing in me—as a writer and as a photographer. We have created something truly beautiful together! Your guidance and enthusiasm along the way as I navigated writing my first cookbook were priceless.

To Cara, my project manager, thank you for your attention to every detail and your overall commitment to make this book the absolute best it could be.

To Danny, thank you for your intense pickiness when it comes to food. *(Never thought I'd say that!)* You helped make this book better, tasting and providing feedback on every recipe, and guaranteeing that if you liked it, almost anyone would. There were some intense weeks, with probably more kale than a vegetable-hater like you would prefer to eat at a time, and yet you supported me gracefully. Thank you for your willingness to incorporate more superfoods into your diet, all in the name of health. And, thank you for letting me borrow (and get Greek yogurt on) your camera!

To Babycakes, thank you for inspiring me to be my healthiest and happiest self. You are so strong, smart, and beautiful, my dear. I really can't say I love you enough. I love you. I love you. I LOVE YOU!!!! I want to constantly smother your neck with kisses, sing you a thousand "Twinkle Twinkles," and celebrate who you become. You make my heart full.

To Mom, thank you for being my biggest cheerleader! Thanks for truly caring about every detail in this entire book as much as I do. I couldn't have done it without you. I can't wait to have you living so close by so that we can enjoy these recipes together, over a glass of wine!

To Dad, thank you for instilling in me a genuine passion and enthusiasm for good food, teaching me that the sky's the limit when it comes to what I can accomplish, equipping me with the "WIN—what's important now" strategy so that I could juggle writing a book, raising a toddler, and working part time successfully. Last, but not least, thank you for telling me daily how proud you are of me. It means the world to me.

To Shannon, thank you for letting me bounce ideas off you from day one, sharing in my excitement when I landed the deal, testing so many recipes, proofing page upon page, and living/breathing this process by my side.

To Katie and Beth, thank you for encouraging me to pursue my personal passions and creating an environment in which that is valuable. And during those months when the cookbook writing was at its most intense, thank you for your understanding when I was a bit disheveled, divided, and distracted.

To Patty, Claire, Melanie, and Hannah, thank you for being my most favorite taste-testers! Every day I would see the biggest smiles on your faces when I walked through that door with new recipes to try. Thank you for your honest feedback, your thousand "thank you's" and "I love you's," and your enthusiasm to see what I was cooking up next. You really helped me stay motivated and focused throughout the entire process.

To my *Nosh and Nourish* blog readers, please accept my utmost thanks for the all of the support, enthusiasm, and excitement you've given me over the past two years. Each comment, vote, and email was so valuable to me. You are why I am here today, finishing up the acknowledgments for my actual printed cookbook! Thank you for all your patience waiting for this book to be completed. I can't wait for it to be in your hands and in your kitchens! I hope you love these new recipes as much as I do.

about the author

For the first thirty years of her life, Kelly Pfeiffer didn't enjoy, er . . . *hated* cooking. She often found herself in the kitchen in the middle of cooking realizing she was missing an important ingredient . . . like making Honey Dijon Chicken and discovering she didn't have any mustard! The shift came when she realized she much preferred looking in the pantry, seeing what was on hand, and creating something from scratch rather than trying to follow someone else's recipe. And in doing so, she discovered she was quite talented in creating delicious, unique, and nourishing recipes, and that she actually enjoyed it! In March 2012, Kelly started the blog *Nosh and Nourish* to showcase her recipes and exquisite food photography and inspire others to live a happy, healthy life. Her goal is to make healthy eating seem doable in the hustle and bustle of everyday life. Her food/recipes have been featured in *Fox News Magazine, Cosmopolitan, Harper's Bazaar, Elle, Country Living, Parade* magazine, the *Saturday Evening Post,* and *Boston* magazine. She is a regular contributor to the Huffington Post, www.RebootwithJoe.com, and www.Skinnymom.com, and periodically teaches a middle school class called Nourishing Snacks. When not creating new recipes or taking pictures of them, she can be found exploring the mountains, gardening, hiking, or fly-fishing. She and her husband live with their toddler and two beagles in a small mountain town outside of Denver. Kelly's blog can be found at www.noshandnourish.com.

index